G
THRC
WITH GOD

A 150 DAY JOURNEY WITH ELISHA

Philip J Seifert

ISBN: 978-1-7392018-1-4

First published in the United Kingdom in 2023 by Malkosh Press.
Printed in the United Kingdom by Book Vault, Peterborough.
Front cover original photo by 'Balazs Toth' @dream perfection.
Cover photo accessed and edited with wording using Canva Pro.
Back cover design template by Dynamik_design1 (Fiverr.com).

Orders for this book can be placed through the following website:
www.malkoshpress.co.uk
Contact with the author can be made through the following email address: info@malkoshpress.co.uk

In accordance with the Legal Deposit Libraries Act 2003, a print copy of this book has been sent to the British Library.

Christmas 2023.

May God bless and encourage you as you read this book

Nana and Papa

Dedication

I wish to dedicate this book to my loving wife, Edneide (Di).

'Who can find a virtuous woman?
for her price is far above rubies.'

Proverbs 31:10

Contents

Introduction

In my mind I can hear a spaghetti western tune playing as a mysterious figure approaches a farm from the distance. He throws his cloak onto a man who is ploughing and walks on without speaking a word. This is 'prophet code' for: *'A call has been placed on your life. Will you accept it?'* Elisha runs after his new mentor, Elijah, and never looks back. There is a price to be paid. He will say goodbye to his family and turn his back on a successful farming business, but Elisha is determined to *go through with God.*

Going through with God is never easy. There are temptations that come our way, disappointments, discouragements, obstacles, battles, and so many other things that can easily knock us off course. On the front cover of this book, the fire represents the trials that come our way as we seek to *go through with God.* As the figure is seen running towards the cross, so we must run to Jesus and hide in Him, resting on what He has done for us at Calvary.

What does it mean to *go through with God?* It can actually mean a number of things.

1. It can be speaking of that moment when we first came to Jesus for salvation. There were different people, various circumstances and even our own thoughts which held us back, but we *went through with Jesus* and began that journey.

2. Although salvation is a one-off experience, yet there is that aspect where we must make a daily decision to *follow through with Jesus.* The Lord said that we have to take up our cross *daily* and follow Him (Luke 9:23). Again, there will be different forces at work which try to hinder us.

3. God doesn't bless us according to our 'performance,' but by His grace, yet we still should hunger, thirst and seek to *go through with Him.* I know of a minister (non-Pentecostal) who determined with two other friends to 'pray through' for more power in their ministries. They kept on their knees for the most of one or two

days (including through the night). Then suddenly, as God's power fell on them, breakthrough came, and they testified that their walk with God and power in their ministries were never the same since that day.

4. *Going through with God* can include those times when we know God is asking us to do something for Him. Sometimes, we draw back and need encouraged to *go through with it.*

There are, no doubt, many other scenarios you can think of. Maybe we need to take a stand for God in some area of our lives. Perhaps we need more power in prayer, passion for the lost or insights into our Bible study. It could be that we need to be freed from religiosity and to have a closer, personal walk with Jesus. Keep seeking the Lord for these things. You will notice one recurring theme is to ask, seek and knock. *Go through with God.*

This book is for anyone. If you are not a Christian, I trust this will encourage you to take that initial first step through repentance and faith in Jesus (see Page 179). If you are a backslider, I pray this book will be used to bring you back to the place you should be. If, however, you are *going through with God*, you will still need encouragement to keep going on despite the fiery trials that come your way. This book will also encourage you to put your arm around someone else who may be struggling and inspire them to *go through with God.*

Finally, I apologise for the personal illustrations throughout the book, but using outside-sourced illustrations causes a lot of copyright 'headaches.' Thank you to those who allowed me to include their stories. Any profit made from this book after costs have been covered will go to Donaghcloney Elim Church Building Fund.

I'm going through, yes, I'm going through;

I'll pay the price, whatever others do;

I'll take the way of my Lord's despised few;

I've started in Jesus, and I'm going through.

Herbert Buffman [1]

SECTION 1

ELISHA'S CALL

1st Kings 19:19-21

DAY 1

Pass It On

For whatsoever things were written beforetime were written
for our learning, that we through patience
and comfort of the scriptures might have hope.
Romans 15:4

I learned a lot from my Granny McKinley. She initially taught me how to play the piano and was the first brave person to try to teach me how to drive a car. I can only imagine her panic on the first lesson as I thrust the gear stick into reverse instead of forward, almost hitting a telegraph pole. I also have memories of her kneeling beside the bed and praying (with Lynne and myself on either side). I am told that on one occasion, after a few minutes of prayer, I impatiently said, *'Granny, say Amen and get up'!*

As we come to study Elisha, you may ask what we can learn from a Bible character who lived around the 9th century B.C.? How can his life, from such a long time ago, have any bearing on ours today in the 21st century A.D.?

Well, just as my Grandmother passed down her skills to another generation, today's verse reminds us that these Bible stories were written not just to give us something nice to read but, more importantly, that each generation may learn something from them.

The situations that Elisha faced are similar in a way to ours today. He lived in a politically corrupt world. His nation had once been God-fearing, but that was no longer true. As we study the life of Elisha, we will observe how his faith shines through even in the most corrupt of societies. Difficult circumstances did not stifle the work that he had been called to do. Impossibilities were met with a steadfast faith in God that could move mountains.

Let us be thankful today that we can hold the precious Word of God in our hands. It is a Bible college in itself, and we can learn daily from its godly tutors. Paul says these things were written so that we should have patience and hope. As we study them, let us also pass this hope on to the next generation.

DAY 2

For A Time Like This

Elias was a man subject to like passions as we are, and he prayed earnestly that it might not rain: and it rained not on the earth by the space of three years and six months.
James 5:17

'*Cometh the hour, cometh the man'* (or woman)! When slavery was rife worldwide, William Wilberforce arose as a champion of the oppressed in his day. When disease seemed unstoppable, Marie Curie changed the world of medicine with her pioneering ideas. During Britain's darkest night, Sir Winston Churchill stepped up and became the symbol of dogged determination as he rallied the nation along the road to victory.

We can find a similar pattern in the Bible. God always raises His people to do great and mighty things in the darkest days. Even as Jacob and his family faced famine, God was already working through Joseph in Egypt to provide for His people. As enslaved Hebrews groaned under the burdens of their taskmasters, a little crying baby floating along the Nile River would soon be used by God to set His people free. As a sinful world headed towards destruction and ruin, a Saviour walked up Calvary's hill and would pay the price to free the guilty. God always has His man or woman ready, even in the worst times.

Elijah and Elisha were two such men whom God raised in a period of great political corruption and religious apostasy. Things were so bad at one stage that Elijah thought he was the only one in the land who was standing for God. Yet he soon learned that seven thousand still hadn't bowed the knee to Baal (1st Kings 19:18).

It is so easy for us to become discouraged today as well. But God is raising people in these difficult times. He is raising His Elijahs, Elishas, Deborahs, and Esthers for a time like this. Go and be one in your community, family, workplace or church. Who knows what God is raising you to do for Him at this time? *Go through with God* and make a difference today.

DAY 3

Unqualified?

So he departed from there, and found Elisha the son of Shaphat, who was ploughing with twelve yoke of oxen before him, and he with the twelfth: 1st Kings 19:19a

Would you tell your health problems to a doctor who had never studied medicine? Would you take your car to be fixed by someone who didn't know the difference between the engine and the boot of a car? Yet here we have Elijah going to visit the man whom God has appointed his successor, and as far as we can tell, he is unqualified to be a prophet (although Elijah will become his mentor). At this time, there was a *school* or a *group of prophets* with whom it seems Elisha had no connection.

God has a habit of choosing those we would not even consider while often passing over those we think are the best qualified. If you had the job of selecting twelve disciples, would you have wandered down to a few fishing boats to recruit rough and unlearned men? Would you have chosen a tax collector who was hated by his people? Would you have appointed as their leader Peter, a man who usually forgot to put his mind into gear before he put his mouth into motion?

Why would Elijah be sent to a guy ploughing on farmland, who seems utterly unqualified as his successor? I think the answer can be found in 1st Corinthians 1:27-29 which tells us that God chooses the foolish, weak, lowly, and despised things of this world to confuse those who are seen as wise and mighty. When that happens, *God is glorified and no one else.*

Maybe today, you feel weak, unimportant, and even useless for the Kingdom of God. Hold that thought right there. That is the type of person God is most likely to use. On recognising our weakness before God, what we do with that imperfection is so important. When we place *our weaknesses* entirely in His hands, God can take over with *His power* and *His strength.* Why not do that today and see what He will achieve through you for His glory?

DAY 4

Mundane Moments

.....who was ploughing with twelve yoke of oxen before him,
and he with the twelfth:
1st Kings 19:19b

I remember when God was moving in my heart regarding attending Bible college and I was exploring if there was a specific work that He had for me to do. It was 2012, and we had just returned from a holiday in Portugal, where Di's mum lives. Her brother, Aroldo, is a Pastor there, and one day, as he drove us from a church service, I felt God was stirring something in my heart. From that time onwards, I felt very unsettled in my workplace. In June of that year, Pastor Sydney Kerr spoke in Lisburn Elim church on the apostle Paul's words, 'Lord, What would you have me to do?' (Acts 9:6). It was like an arrow to my heart, and I felt the Lord was indeed calling me to do something for Him. But it was initially while on a relaxing holiday in Portugal, I first sensed God moving in my heart about this matter.

You see, God speaks to us in the mundane moments of life. God spoke to Moses while he was tending sheep and to Gideon as he was threshing wheat. Matthew was called by Jesus while collecting taxes. Peter was casting a net while James and John were mending nets. Jesus spoke with a Samaritan woman as she drew water from a well. Jacob met God as he slept on a stone, which he used as a pillow. God meets with us in the daily routine of our lives.

The call came to Elisha as he was ploughing fields. He was just going about his everyday business. There was no angel choir, inspiring speech, shaking mountain, burning bush, ladders from Heaven, dreams or visions. On one occasion, God came to his predecessor Elijah in a still, small voice instead of the wind, earthquake or fire. Why do we often seem to expect a bright light or something dramatic when we encounter God? He awaits you while driving the car, brushing up the leaves in the garden, lying in a hospital bed, drinking a mug of coffee, or wiping a tear from your eye. Listen for His voice today.

DAY 5

The Challenge

.......and Elijah passed by him, and cast his mantle upon him.
1st Kings 19:19b

The call of Elisha is almost theatrical. I can imagine him looking up and seeing a mysterious figure approaching from afar. The Bible doesn't describe any dialogue between the two, which makes it even more intriguing. As Elijah gets closer to Elisha, he throws down his prophet's mantle onto Elisha and walks on. The mantle signified Elijah's authority as a prophet.[2] In effect, he challenges Elisha to pick it up and become his successor. This event has got to be one of the strangest calls to serve God in the Bible. How will Elisha respond to this challenge?

When God calls, He wants a response. Various Bible characters have responded in different ways to their call. Isaiah stood in that Holy place surrounded by seraphim, and as the smoke arose and the door posts shook, the voice of the Lord rang out, '*Whom shall I send, and who shall go for us?'* Isaiah's reply was immediate: *'Here am I'* (Isaiah 6:8).

Moses stood in another Holy place: for him, it was a burning bush. As he removed his sandals from that Holy ground, he received a call from God. Moses doubted his ability and questioned, *'Who am I?'* (Exodus 3:11).

Jonah (to use a pun) was a *different kettle of fish.* When called by God to preach to Nineveh, He didn`t say, *'Here am I'* or *'Who am I?'* but he might as well have said, *'Where am I?'* as he played hide and seek with God and went on the run (Jonah 1:3). How will Elisha respond? We will have a look later.

We all receive calls of some sort from God. It may not be to go across the world as a missionary or to be a pastor or worship leader. It may be to cross the road and tell someone about Jesus, help in church, or phone someone who is lonely. In what way is God calling you? How will you respond? Don't run like Jonah or doubt like Moses, but say like Isaiah, *'Here am I.'*

DAY 6

At The Crossroads

And he left the oxen.....
1st Kings 19:20a

We all come at some stage to a crossroads in life, which can often shape our future. Granny McKinley had a friend named Jack, who, as a young man, was at a crossroads in his life. He had been attending gospel meetings and was concerned about his soul, but there was a specific direction that his life was taking. He most likely would have been led away from God if he continued in it. My Grandmother wrote him a letter, which quoted John 3:16, substituting Jack's name into the verse: *'For God so loved Jack, etc.'* As a result of that letter, Jack gave his life to Jesus and became a missionary for over forty years in the West Indies.

As Elisha stands at *his* crossroads, he cannot hold onto the plough and follow Elijah simultaneously. He has a choice to make. Jesus spoke in Luke 14:28 about counting the cost. There is a cost to discipleship. There is a cost to following Jesus. It is thought that because Elisha was ploughing with twelve yokes of oxen, he came from a comfortable (if not wealthy) background.[3] To follow Elijah, he will have to leave it all behind.

Our *church motto text* for this year has been Matthew 6:33, which instructs us to seek the Kingdom of God first and His righteousness. Seeking God first will mean that there are other things in our lives we will have to view as lower priorities. Jesus never dressed discipleship up as being easy. He was upfront about it and told us it involved taking up our cross daily (Luke 9:23). However, when viewed in the light of the peace that comes through knowing Jesus down here and of our future in Heaven, the cost is minimal compared to the glory that awaits us.

You may stand at a crossroads today. Are you being called to follow Jesus, or are you being called into a closer walk with Himself? Count the cost, and put Jesus first. You will not regret it.

DAY 7

Running After God

……and ran after Elijah
1st Kings 19:20b

It was December 19th, 2006. I texted my (then) girlfriend (Di, now my wife) and told her to *dress up* because I was taking her out for a meal. I arrived with flowers, and I think she was beginning to get a bit suspicious. We went to *Belfast Castle* and had a lovely meal. As we were walking out, I ushered Di into a side room, got down on one knee, read out a mini-speech (written on a piece of paper about the size of a postage stamp), and asked her to marry me. Initially, Di laughed (she claims it was due to nervousness!) That didn't help my confidence, but then she said, *'Yes!'* A group of complete strangers emerged from a nearby elevator, and we excitedly told them our news. You can imagine that we were filled with enthusiasm and joy.

We should not overlook the fact that Elisha *ran after Elijah*. Just as Di and I were excited and enthusiastic about our decision that night, so was Elisha. *He wanted this*. He was in no doubt about it. Nothing was going to stand between Elisha and his calling.

It was similar for the disciples of Jesus. We read that they left their nets and followed Him. They turned their backs on their whole way of living without even a second thought.

It is amazing to read about the many people who run in the Bible, denoting their enthusiasm. As the prodigal son came home, his dad ran to meet him. Zacchaeus ran ahead of Jesus so he could get up a tree to see Him better. Peter ran to the garden tomb on that Resurrection morning. A poor man filled with demon spirits, when he saw Jesus, ran and worshipped Him.

It's lovely to see people run after Jesus, enthusiastically worshipping and following Him. When did you last run after the Lord? Maybe you have lost a bit of that passion recently. Life can do that to us so easily. Come into His presence. Focus on Him. The Holy Spirit will stir up that flame in your heart once again.

DAY 8

No Turning Back

And he returned back from him, and took a yoke of oxen, and slew them,
and boiled their flesh with the instruments of the oxen,
and gave to the people, and they did eat.
1st Kings 19:21a

Most of us have done it. We have been given a box of chocolates during Christmas, and in the New Year have resolved to be very good. Perhaps we placed the sweets high up in a cupboard, literally out of harm's way. But each time we walk past that hiding place, there is a strong temptation to break our New Year resolution. Maybe we will resist for a few days, but soon, the inevitable happens. If only we had given them away to someone else, the problem would have been solved. *Knowing they were there proved to be too much of a temptation.*

In verse 20, Elisha requests to go back to say goodbye to his parents. He does so and turns his back entirely on his old way of life. Previously, we had been told that Elisha was ploughing with twelve yokes of oxen and steering the twelfth pair at the time of his call. In verse 21, he kills a yoke of oxen (probably the ones he had been steering), cooks their meat, gives it to the people, and burns his plough. Elisha is indicating his determination to never return from the new path he has embarked on. Today, we would say that he was burning his bridges. He had *crossed the Rubicon* and was at the point of no return. You see (just like the chocolates), if Elisha had left his plough intact, there would always be the temptation to return if things didn't work out. Now, there is no turning back. He has removed the temptation.

When we first came to Jesus, no doubt there was that desire to follow Him and never turn back. But as time passes, we may be tempted (like Lot's wife) to look back. You see, she hadn't *burned all her bridges*. Part of her was still in Sodom. I wonder today, is God calling us (like Elisha) to *burn our bridges* and serve Him wholeheartedly? *Go through with God.* With the help of the Holy Spirit, keep moving forward with Jesus. No rear-view mirrors!

DAY 9

Get Up And Go

Then he arose, and went after Elijah……
1st Kings 19:21b

'Girls, go and tidy your room.' 'Yes, Dad.'* Thirty minutes pass. *'Girls, I thought I told you to tidy your room.' 'Yes, Dad, we are going to do it now.'* You get the picture, don't you? They promise to do something but never seem to follow through with it. Jesus told a parable about two sons. One told his father he would *not* go and work in his vineyard but repented and obeyed. The other son promised to work in the vineyard but never followed through.

Elisha not only decides to *go through with God* but also *follows through* with his decision. He returned home to say goodbye to his folks, but then *'He arose, and went after Elijah.'* It reminds me of the prodigal son. He had it all worked out in his head. He would go home and tell his father that he had sinned and was only worthy to be treated as a hired servant. That was good. But he could have sat in the pigsty, just dreaming about going home. Then we read that *'He arose, and came to his father'* (Luke 15:20). He followed through with his decision. I wonder how many prodigals have realised the awful place they are in. They know a loving Heavenly Father is waiting to welcome them home with open arms. But they have never *followed through*. They have never come to that place which the prodigal reached where *he arose.* Today is a golden opportunity to arise and return to the arms of your loving Father. Maybe you aren't a prodigal, but know in your heart that you need to reconcile with someone. Will you get up and *follow through?*

Elisha knew God had a work for him to do, and he got up and went for it. Maybe there is something that God has been speaking about to you, but you never seem to get around to doing it. It could be you are worried about the outcome or are simply putting it off. That vision which God has given you will remain dormant until you get up and *follow through*. Will you, like Elisha, arise and go after whatever the Lord is calling you to do? *Go through with God.*

DAY 10

A Servant's Heart

....and ministered to him.
1st Kings 19:21c

There is a café that I would frequent, where a gentleman usually greets you as you come in and helps you find a seat. When you place your order at the counter, he offers to carry your tray over to the table. Now and again, he checks to see if you want your tea or coffee topped up. When he is not doing these things, he is usually chatting with the customers. This gentleman basically does everything he can to make you feel at home and enjoy your experience. I recently discovered that the person in question is actually the owner of the café. I looked up the café on a review website. Some reviewers knew he was the owner; others just referenced 'a kind man,' but almost everyone mentioned him. He is the *owner* of the café but has a *servant's heart.*

On an even grander scale, it is incredible to think that the *Creator* of this world has a *servant's heart.* Jesus came to serve and minister to others (Mark 10:45). Can you imagine the faces of the disciples as Jesus began to wash their feet? Here is God the Son, serving His creation. If we want to be like Jesus, then it is imperative that we have servant hearts.

As Elisha obeys the call upon his life to be Elijah's successor, he isn't paraded with great fanfare among the school of prophets. He doesn`t give an acceptance speech outlining where he sees '*Elisha Ministries'* being in the next twenty years. He doesn't call fire down from Heaven or defeat an army. Instead, Elisha goes and *ministers to Elijah.* He serves. It is thought that for the next six or so years, Elisha faithfully served his mentor,[4] and when Elijah was gone, he just kept faithfully serving God and others. He started the way he meant to continue.

Jesus indicated that the pathway to greatness is found when we become the servant of others (Matthew 20:26). Maybe you will come across a situation in your life today and find yourself asking, *'What would Jesus do?'* Be assured that Jesus would serve.

SECTION 2

PASSING ON THE MANTLE

2nd Kings 2:1-14

DAY 11

Transition

And it came to pass, when the LORD would take up Elijah into heaven by a whirlwind, that Elijah went with Elisha from Gilgal.
2nd Kings 2:1

'*The end of an era.*' When we use that term, we usually mean things won't be the same again. It was used after the passing of Queen Elizabeth II on 8th September, 2022. I heard people recall how, during her seventy-year reign, she had always been there throughout various periods of their lives. For many, the transition to a new king was a daunting prospect. As we know from many walks of life, when someone popular moves on from a position they have held for many years, it can be challenging for the new incumbent to fill their shoes.

The time was approaching when the great prophet Elijah would be taken up into Heaven. The pinnacle of his time as a prophet would probably be seen as that moment when he called down fire from Heaven, defeating four hundred and fifty prophets of Baal. (Reminding us that one plus God is a majority, no matter how many are against you). How could anyone follow in his footsteps? Who could replace Elijah? God had His own man, Elisha, waiting in the wings. He was different in many ways from his mentor, but *the God of Elijah would still be the God of Elisha.* The people had nothing to fear in this transition. In fact, if you count for yourself, the Bible records almost twice as many miracles performed by God through Elisha than his predecessor.

We will always have to deal with change and transition. As the world seems to become more evil daily and we mourn the passing of great men and women of God, we can be tempted to think that things will never be the same again. But take heart. God has His men and women waiting in the wings. God has His Elishas waiting to grab the baton from His Elijahs. *The God of yesterday's generation will still be the God of tomorrow's generation.* It may be the end of an era but also the beginning of an exciting new one.

DAY 12

Testing, Testing, 1,2,3.....

And Elijah said to Elisha, Tarry here, I pray you;
for the LORD has sent me to Bethel.
2nd Kings 2:2a

When I was a small boy, I was unhappy on one particular occasion as I hadn't got my own way over something (probably insignificant). My parents were in the main room, and visitors were with them. I stood at the front door and loudly announced, *'OK. That's it. I'm leaving home. Bye!'* I opened the door and banged it closed but remained inside the house to gauge the reaction. *Silence.* I did it again. *'OK. I'm really away this time!' BANG! Silence.* I was testing to see what my parents would do, but they were playing me at my own game, knowing I had no intention of leaving!

Elijah is going to leave this Earth, and from verse 3, we learn that Elisha and the prophets are aware of this. Before he is caught up to Heaven, he stops at Gilgal, Bethel and Jericho with the other prophets, probably to encourage them before he goes. On each occasion, Elijah says he will be moving on to the next location and that Elisha should remain where he is. But on each of those three occasions, Elisha refuses to let Elijah out of his sight. We aren't told the reasoning behind all of this, but it seems Elijah is putting him to the test. As Elijah's successor, will he stay with him all the way to the very end? Is he really committed to his new calling? Will he *go through with God?*

There is no doubt that at some stage, we will be tested on the things we say and believe. Peter boasted that he would always stand by Jesus. *He was tested on that.* Job 1:1 tells us that Job feared the Lord. *He was tested on that, also.* In school, a test is necessary to evaluate where we are at, and 1st Peter 1:7 explains that testing proves the genuineness of our faith. Be encouraged, though. Testing does not come to trip us up, but Peter goes on to say that the intended outcome is praise, honour and glory when Jesus returns. Failing a test, however, isn`t final. *Ask Peter.*

DAY 13

Determination

And he said, As the LORD lives, and as your soul lives,
I will not leave you. And they two went on.
2nd Kings 2:6b

Have you ever queued up outside the shops all night in an effort to snap up something at the *Boxing Day* sales? Have you worked hard to obtain an academic qualification? Have you diligently excelled in your workplace in order to gain a promotion? Do you remember the first time you set your eyes on your true love and determined that you would win their heart? You see, if there is something that *we really want*, we do everything in our power to get that thing. We go in for it with all of our hearts.

If what we looked at yesterday was indeed a test, there was no way Elisha was going to let Elijah out of his sight. Why was it so important? As we have seen, Elisha knew that Elijah was going to be taken away by the Lord. There were three good reasons that Elisha should be with Elijah until the end. Firstly, on a relational level, out of faithfulness to his mentor. Secondly, when great men of God left this Earth, they often gave some sort of blessing. Lastly, Elijah still had his prophet's mantle, and surely there would be some sort of passing on of the baton. Had Elisha remained at Gilgal, Bethel or Jericho, it may have indicated that the mantle and a blessing were not things he desired with all his heart.

If we really want to progress spiritually, we must have that determination, hunger and thirst to *go through with God.* Do you want to be filled with the Spirit? Do you want to go deeper with God? Do you need a breakthrough? Although everything that we receive from God is lavished upon us by His grace and not through our 'performance' or effort, there is also that aspect which Jesus speaks of where we have to ask, seek, knock (Luke 11:9-13), and desire to put the Kingdom of God first (Matthew 6:33). Jacob wrestled and would not let go until he received the blessing (Genesis 32:26). *Go through with God.* Seek Him with all your heart (Psalm 119:10). This is the road to blessing.

DAY 14

Spectating From The Stands

And fifty men of the sons of the prophets went, and stood to view afar off:
2nd Kings 2:7a

A breaking news item flashes across the TV screen, and in a few seconds, we have dissected the whole situation from the comfort of our armchair, proclaiming exactly how it should be handled. At the end of a football match, along with the TV pundits, we criticise and analyse wrong moves made by the players while we relax on the sofa with a packet of crisps. We have become a nation of spectators. For the spectator, there is a certain comfort in observing from the stands, which protects us from the sweat and struggles of the participants on the field.

It happens in church, too. We watch others sing, pray and preach; then we give our critical analysis at *full-time* around the kitchen table. At other times, we offer our views on what is wrong with the church while drinking a soothing latte. But we do it from *afar off.* We observe, but we don't get involved ourselves. That would be too messy.

As Elijah and Elisha move on from Jericho, they stand at the River Jordan. There are also fifty *sons of the prophets*, and they are spectating *'afar off.'* It reminds us of Peter, who, as Jesus was being led to appear before Caiaphas (the high priest), was following *'afar off'* (Matthew 26:58). It would have been too messy to be seen with Jesus, so he spectated from a distance. As Elijah and Elisha walked into the unknown and God was going to somehow take the great prophet away, I wonder if these fifty men thought it was too risky to go any farther. God's ways are so unpredictable that maybe it was safer to watch from a distance.

Aren't you glad that when Jesus saw our plight as sinners, He didn't spectate from Heaven but came right into our mess and went to Calvary? Today, He calls us from our armchairs and sofas to get involved in the world's mess around us. The Christian life is not a spectator sport but an arena for battle. We aren't called to comfort, but the rallying cry is *'Go into all the world.'*

DAY 15

Crossing The Line Into Victory

.....and they two stood by Jordan.
2nd Kings 2:7b

It is quite clear that when it comes to symbolism, the River Jordan speaks of a boundary line that can be crossed. *'The other side of the River Jordan'* and similar wording is often used in the Bible. Crossing the Jordan is also linked to victory, as it was there God's people entered the Promised Land.

A seasoned prophet and a rookie walk side by side as they journey to cross a boundary line that will bring them to a place of victory. Elisha has pressed on in order to get to this place. He could have stopped at Gilgal, Bethel, or Jericho but refused to and pushed forward. When Elisha crosses this line, he will receive a much-needed anointing for the coming days. Elijah will be one of only two men (three if you count Melchizedek in Hebrews 7:3) who never died and will be caught up into Heaven through a whirlwind.

I have always been a very quiet person. As someone who previously had to turn down giving a best man's speech at a friend's wedding, anything public was almost impossible. After I was saved, I could not pray in public or give my testimony. However, I had been pressing in with God for some time. Suddenly (one evening in the front room of our house), I felt as if a fresh, powerful fire had been lit up in my spirit as I contemplated what Jesus had done on the cross for me. A short time later, I remember praying for the first time out loud in a prayer meeting and giving my testimony in church. For me, these were massive steps. It seemed I had *crossed over a boundary line into victory.*

Going through with God can be difficult. It involves having our eyes fixed on a goal and walking that straight line while ignoring the things in the way that will try to turn us aside. As I've stated elsewhere, while the victory doesn't depend on our 'performance' but rather God's grace, He does promise to satisfy the hungry soul (Psalm 107:9). Keep pressing towards that line. You will cross over by His grace, and victory will be yours.

DAY 16

Until The End

And Elijah took his mantle, and wrapped it together, and smote the waters, and they were divided here and there, so that they two went over on dry ground.
2nd Kings 2:8

Captain Scott 'of the Antarctic' was last known to be attempting to fulfil his dream of reaching the South Pole. We know that he and his team tragically died on their return journey. Amelia Earhart was last known to be attempting to become the first woman to fly around the world. It seems she died in her attempt, although her body was never found. These are just two examples of people who were actively pursuing a goal and giving their all towards it the last time they were seen alive.

Elijah was about to leave this Earth. He knew it was his last day and was ready to go. If you knew today was going to be your last day, are you ready to go? The last that Elijah was seen, he was still pursuing his goal of *going through with God.* He had some blips along the way (as we all do). He had almost given up at one stage, but God gave him the strength to get up again. On Elijah's last day, he was still fulfilling his calling and pursuing God's will. Until the end, he was still performing miracles as he parted the River Jordan. Until the end, his final concerns were about his successor, Elisha, and that he would be equipped to continue the work of God. As God took him to Heaven in a whirlwind, the last Elijah was seen, he was still running the race.

Until the end, Jesus was seeking sinners. Even while on the cross, He promised a dying criminal a place in Heaven. Until the end, Paul said he had fought the good fight, finished the course and kept the faith (2nd Timothy 4:7). Until the end, Stephen was "full of the Holy Ghost" (Acts 7:55) and forgiving those who were stoning him to death. As a pastor, when taking part in a funeral service, it is such a blessing to be able to confidently testify about the deceased that the last they were seen, they were *going through with God.* Keep running the race.

DAY 17

What Do You Really Want?

And it came to pass, when they were gone over, that Elijah said to Elisha, Ask what I shall do for you, before I be taken away from you.
2nd Kings 2:9a

When we go into town with the kids, we know they will eventually see something they desire. Of course, there is nothing in the world quite like whatever it is they want us to buy. Assurances are made that if we buy it for them, they will never ask for anything ever again (at least for the next day or so!) This toy, so vital to their happiness, can sometimes be discarded in a few days and never played with again. It is sometimes difficult to distinguish between need and greed!

Here, Elisha is basically being given a blank cheque. He is asked by Elijah if there is anything that he wants before he is taken away to Heaven. We will look at his answer tomorrow, but for now, we will stay with this thought of wishes being granted.

In 1st Kings 3:5, King Solomon is told by God that He would grant him whatever he asked. The king was burdened with having to judge disputes that arose in his Kingdom, so he asked for wisdom. God commended him for that, and because Solomon had discerned this to be more important than asking for riches, He would grant both wisdom and riches. Unfortunately, towards the end of his life, Solomon (similar to kids with an unwanted gift) seemed to discard the wisdom he had initially requested.

If God was to grant you the desire of your heart, what would it be? What is important to you? Whatever it is that you would ask for will tell you a lot about your own heart. Solomon's father, David, had a desire *for just one thing*: to dwell in the House of the Lord all his life (Psalm 27:4). The House of the Lord was at that time where the presence of the Lord was. David wanted God's presence more than anything else. David desired to *go through with God.* Jesus said that where our treasure is, our hearts will also be there (Matthew 6:21). What is your treasure?

DAY 18

Our Need For God's Power

And Elisha said, I pray you,
let a double portion of your spirit be upon me.
2nd Kings 2:9b

The home we grew up in had a large hedge around the front, down the side and around the back. The house technically belonged to my Granny McKinley, who laid down the law about cutting the hedge (using hand clippers, not electric ones). I stood looking at the hedge around 8 a.m. one morning. It seemed the task ahead would take forever. I had a half-hour lunch break, the same for dinner, and finished around 8 p.m. that evening. I would have loved to have had the power of the electric clippers; it would have made my task so much easier and quicker.

As Elisha stood on the other side of Jordan, realising his mentor was leaving, he must have been overcome with the task ahead. A couple of days ago, we saw how Elijah had retreated into a cave, ready to give it all up due to discouragement. If that is how the pressure of this wayward nation had affected the mighty prophet, what hope would Elisha have? When Elijah offered to grant whatever Elisha desired, his younger apprentice could have asked for money, knowing that a prophet's life would not be prosperous. But I suspect Elisha saw a greater need than money. He saw the necessity for God's power in his life because he certainly could not do this alone.

It's good to have an honest appraisal of ourselves before God. If the conclusion is that we are weak, imperfect and prone to mistakes, don't despair because it's not all bad news. The acknowledgement of our need should drive us into the arms of God, seeking His help. Are you overwhelmed as you look ahead and see the task before you? God's strength is made perfect in our weakness (2nd Corinthians 12:9). Using my own power and ability hampered my work on the hedge. I required greater power from an outside source. Ask God's Spirit to energise you with power today.

DAY 19

The Double Portion

And Elisha said, I pray you,
let a double portion of your spirit be upon me.
2nd Kings 2:9b

Elisha asks Elijah for a double portion of his spirit. What does that mean? The Bible records around twice as many miracles performed by Elisha than by his mentor. Is this what he is asking for? It seems this is not necessarily the case. Deuteronomy 21:17 tells of the double portion the firstborn son would receive from his father's inheritance. By inheriting Elijah's mantle, Elisha is his 'firstborn' and requires a spiritual inheritance passed on from his spiritual father. Considering the magnitude of the task before him, Elisha needs to walk in Elijah's authority and anointing. If Elijah required it, then Elisha reckoned he needed it too, and more.

Had Jesus given the disciples the commission to go into all the world and preach the gospel without any promise of help, they surely would have been overwhelmed with the task. But Jesus told them that before they were to do anything at all, they were to wait for power from on High in the form of the Holy Spirit (Acts 1:4,8). It must have been a relief to know that God would supply the power they needed.

Whatever our denominational backgrounds may be, surely we will acknowledge the necessity for the power of God in our lives to carry out the assignments He has given us. For Pentecostals, it is the *Baptism in the Holy Ghost*. For some, it is the *Second Blessing*, while for others, it is the *infilling of the Spirit*. I'm not going to get into a theological debate about this; you will be glad to know! All I will say is that whatever you believe in, *you need it! I need it!* Whatever your theological persuasion, seek the power that you require. We are nothing without the power of the Spirit of God. The need around us is great, but the power available is *far greater*. Realising his inadequacy, Elisha simply asked for that power and received it. Why not ask for His power today?

DAY 20

How Bold Are You?

And he said, You have asked a hard thing: nevertheless,
if you see me when I am taken from you, it shall be so to you;
but if not, it shall not be so.
2nd Kings 2:10

When Granny McKinley went shopping (having seen some clothes she liked), she would nearly always ask the shop assistant if they could *'knock a few pounds off the price!'* Mum used to be so embarrassed by this all the time. But *'if you don't ask, you don't get.'* The crux of the matter is whether you are bold enough to ask the question!

When Elisha asks for a double portion of Elijah's spirit, it seems that the boldness of his request shocks his mentor. He replies that it is a hard thing which Elisha is asking. Elijah then informs Elisha how he will know if his request has been granted.

Although the shop assistants were probably stunned by Granny's request, it seems that God is not shocked by our bold petitions. Abraham boldly bargained with God over Sodom, asking for it to be spared according to how many righteous people lived there (Genesis 18:16-33). Abraham actually brings the figure down from fifty to ten. I wonder what would have happened if he had bargained for five? But he stopped. Moses boldly interceded for his people when they had sinned. He told God to kill him, too, if He was going to punish them. Moses lived to tell the tale. Hezekiah pleaded for more years to be added to his life. A Gentile woman who knew that her people were looked upon as dogs by the Jews dared to ask Jesus to heal her daughter.

Abraham's pleading wasn`t enough because there weren`t ten righteous people in Sodom, but at least he tried. Imagine the consequences if Moses, Hezekiah and this Gentile woman had been silent. Surely, it is better to ask God for something that seems too big than not to ask at all. The things that seem like huge mountains to us are tiny hills to the Lord. Nothing is impossible with God (Luke 1:37).

DAY 21

A Bonus

And it came to pass, as they still went on, and talked, that, behold, there appeared a chariot of fire, and horses of fire, and parted them both asunder; and Elijah went up by a whirlwind into heaven.
2nd Kings 2:11

I remember hearing (from family) what was said to be a true story about a man who fell asleep in church. At a contemplative moment in the service, when all was quiet, in the middle of his dream, he exclaimed, *'Hurrah! We're Aff!'* For those who do not live in Northern Ireland or do not understand our varying accents, he was, in effect, saying, *'Hooray! We are off!'* (or we are away). In this man's dream, Jesus had returned, and he was expressing his delight that he had been caught up to meet the Lord in the air! The bewildered faces of those looking on may not have so instantaneously understood his random outburst!

While life is never promised to be easy for the Christian, we do know that we have a refuge and strength in God, abundant life in Jesus, the power of the Spirit of God to help us, the encouragement of other believers, and the promise of Heaven. But there is a bonus. The bonus for each generation is that theirs may be the generation which experiences the great event of the return of Jesus. It is called by Paul the *'blessed hope'* (Titus 2:13).

I spoke recently to an elderly widowed believer who, amid her pain and the trials of life, regularly takes comfort in the fact that she may never have to die. As God's people, we are actually instructed to comfort each other with this hope (1st Thessalonians 4:18). I think we should teach and preach this truth more and more. When we neglect to do so, we rob ourselves of a truth meant to encourage us.

Elijah's transport into Heaven is a picture of what lies ahead for a blessed generation which will never see death. We don't know when it will be, but I feel it cannot be far away. Whether we are alive or not when it happens, the dead and living shall both participate in that great event. What a moment that will be.

DAY 22

It's Not Over Until It's Over

And Elisha saw it, and he cried, My father, my father, the chariot of Israel, and the horsemen thereof. And he saw him no more: and he took hold of his own clothes, and rent them in two pieces.
2nd Kings 2:12

I had a special interest in the *Euro 21* soccer tournament, as Switzerland had qualified for the competition. With my Great-grandfather being Swiss, I was keen to see their team do well. They progressed to the knockout stages and were set to play against the mighty French team (the World Cup holders at the time). At one stage, the Swiss were 3-1 down, and it seemed like it was all over. Then, the French were hit by two late goals scored in the 81st and 90th minutes during an exciting Swiss comeback. The nail-biting penalty shootout saw the Swiss knock the French out of the tournament by five penalties to four. The Swiss had looked finished at one stage, but *'It's not over until it's over.'*

This verse tells us that Elisha 'saw him [Elijah] no more' and is noteworthy because Elijah had thought he was 'finished' several years previously. Jezebel had sent word that she would have him killed within twenty-four hours (1st Kings 19:2). She had spoken something over his life, and Elijah believed it. No matter what anyone speaks over your life, *what God speaks over your life matters far more.* Despite what Jezebel had said, this was not Elijah's time to go.

Elijah goes on the run and asks God to take his life. The first threat to his life came from outside, the second from within. Fear and discouragement had brought him to that place. But God had other plans. He looked after His weary servant and sent him back into His work to train Elisha. We aren`t told in the Bible, but it is thought that Elijah and Elisha had around six years together.[5] You see, *'It's not over until it's over.'* Jezebel and Elijah's view of the timing of his death were completely different from God's timing. In fact, Elijah never died! Don't despair. All may look lost for now, but there is always hope with God.

DAY 23

Step Out In Faith

He took up also the mantle of Elijah that fell from him, and went back, and stood by the bank of Jordan; And he took the mantle of Elijah that fell from him, and smote the waters,
2nd Kings 2:13, 14a

Elisha has requested the double portion of Elijah's spirit. Elijah said that if he sees him ascending to Heaven, then his petition has been granted (which it is). Everything seems to have fallen into place, except for one thing: Elisha has to do his part and step out in faith. He won't have long to wait. Soon, he stands once again at the same River Jordan that Elijah parted as his last miracle. If Elisha truly has received the double portion, then he will be able to replicate what Elijah has done. He parts the waters, and the spectating prophets confirm this transition of the mantle by saying, *'The spirit of Elijah does rest on Elisha'* (verse 15).

Before he did all this, we read that Elisha ripped up his own clothes and put on Elijah's mantle. God was moving in a new way in Elisha's life. Do you ever tire of going through the motions in your Christian life? Did you know that God has something fresh for you? He is not a God of *staleness* but a God of *new things*. Maybe He has a new gifting or anointing for you to walk in. But you have to *put it on and walk in it.*

The other thing we must do is learn to step out in faith. As Elisha stands at the Jordan, he can look at it for as long as he wishes, but nothing will happen until he steps out in faith. Elisha has to walk in the new mantle he has been given and the fresh anointing which has fallen upon him. He has to take hold of that mantle and, by faith, strike those waters. By taking this step of faith, he is putting his faith into action. I wonder if God is calling you to take a step of faith and walk in the anointing He has given you. One last thing. Elisha proved what Jesus would later say in Luke 11:9: to a*sk, and you shall receive, seek, and you shall find, knock, and the door shall be opened.* Elisha had been bold enough to do that. Ask in faith, receive by faith, and step out in faith.

DAY 24

Where Is The God Of Elijah?

.....and said, Where is the LORD God of Elijah? and when he had also smitten the waters, they parted here and there: and Elisha went over.
2nd Kings 2:14(b)

I wonder if what I am about to describe has happened to you? The computer is showing a blank screen. You press a few keys on the keyboard randomly. Nothing happens. You remember that sometimes the solution is to restart, and everything will usually be restored. Nothing happens. No matter what you try, the screen is blank. After a while, you realise you are getting nowhere and ask for help. Someone approaches the computer, glances at the socket on the wall, and switches on the power supply! It is moments like these when we want to fade quietly into the background. The point is that although the computer is one of the most significant technological advancements of our time, it can only be of any use if the power supply is switched on.

As the prophet's mantle has been passed on to Elisha, he steps out in faith and asks, *'Where is the God of Elijah?'* Having been granted his request for a double portion of Elijah's spirit, Elisha expects the same power of God which parted the Jordan River for Elijah to now do the same for him as he crosses back over. Someone has pointed out (I cannot remember who) that the order here is important. Elisha strikes the river with the mantle, and the waters are parted. In between those two instances, he calls on the God of Elijah. Why is that so vital? *The power is not in the mantle of Elijah but the God of Elijah.* Yes, he strikes the water with the mantle, but it is only a piece of clothing without the power of God (just as a computer is nothing without a power supply).

We get it very wrong when we think that because of a great move of God in the past through a particular denomination, building, preacher, method, style or song, there is some sort of special power in those things or people. The power comes from God. The Church today needs to take its focus off all these things and declare, *'Where is the God of Elijah?'* It is His power we desperately need.

SECTION 3

DIGGING DITCHES

2nd Kings 3:1-25

DAY 25

Taking Responsibility

And the king of Israel said, Alas! that the LORD has called these three kings together, to deliver them into the hand of Moab!
2nd Kings 3:10

You have had those moments when you think you are ninety-nine per cent right about something, and your spouse (or someone else) thinks they are right. Sometimes, Di will place a challenge. Whoever ends up being wrong may have to take the other person out for a meal, give them breakfast in bed for a week, or do the dishes for a week. Through experience, I have learned to no longer accept those challenges. It usually means that Di knows she is definitely going to win, and I haven't a hope! It's better just to admit I am wrong and skip the challenge.

King Jehoram now rules the Northern Kingdom in the place of his wicked father. Unfortunately, it is a case of *like father, like son.* The news comes that the king of Moab is saying he will no longer pay a tribute of 100,000 lambs and rams (and their wool) to Jehoram. King Jehoram asks King Jehoshaphat (the king of Judah) to go with him to crush this rebellion, and the king of Edom joins them on the way. They journey for seven days through the wilderness and run out of water. Jehoram says that God has called the three of them together to deliver them into the hand of the king of Moab. God is being blamed for something that He had not done! (So often, God seems to get the blame in our lives). We do not read of Jehoram consulting God at all concerning attacking Moab.

Jehoram's best hope in this situation would have been to *man up* and face reality. He had got it wrong. Just call on God and hand it over to Him. But instead, he blames God. Today's word is challenging. If we want to *go through with God*, we must face the realities of our decisions. We do get things wrong, but pride blames someone else. Wrongly blaming others only leads us down a pathway that is not good for us. Alternatively, humbly taking responsibility and seeking God for help opens a path to restoration and healing. Is that what we need to do today?

DAY 26

Desperate Times, Desperate Measures

But Jehoshaphat said, Is there not here a prophet of the LORD, that we may inquire of the LORD by him? And one of the king of Israel's servants answered and said, Here is Elisha the son of Shaphat, which poured water on the hands of Elijah.
2nd Kings 3:11

It is a common saying that there are *few atheists in the trenches*. The sudden prospect of death or danger drives many to their knees. Many of us have heard testimonies where someone promised that if the Lord would bring them through a specific situation, they would *go through with God*. Some fulfilled their promise, while others did not. The Psalms record many instances where David was desperately sent to his knees to cry to God.

Three kings and their armies have been travelling for seven days through the wilderness and have run out of water. The situation is dire. Due to this lack of water, they are facing possible annihilation by their enemies. No doubt driven by his desperation, Jehoshaphat suggests that they seek God through a prophet. Jehoram had initially blamed God, but now there is talk of seeking Him instead. Unfortunately, they hadn't sought Him before they went on their mission, but the important thing is that they are seeking Him now. At least they are moving in the right direction. There is a possibility that God may have mercy on them.

It's a pity that sometimes we have to wait until desperate times come to call on God. When things are going well, the Lord isn't always given the proper place He should have in our lives. But circumstances change, and it drives us to our knees in desperation. Maybe that is where you are at the moment as you read these words. The most important thing right now is that you are seeking the Lord. It has taken adverse circumstances to get you to that place, but you are in the right place now. When we get into that place of desperation and humility and bow our knees before Him, we are in the best possible position. In taking that posture, David found mercy, renewal and deliverance. You can, too.

DAY 27

A Person Of Influence

And Elisha said, As the LORD of hosts lives, before whom I stand, surely, were it not that I regard the presence of Jehoshaphat the king of Judah, I would not look toward you, nor see you.
2nd Kings 3:14

A man named Jackie (with whom I worked at the time) constantly witnessed to me before I was saved. After I got saved, that wasn't the end of it. He repeatedly tried to encourage me to *go through with God*, especially in the area of prayer. He attempted to get me to attend an early morning prayer meeting held in the church at 6:30 a.m. every Friday. I kept putting him off, but he eventually got through to me. I vaguely said I would try to get out sometime when the new season began in the New Year. Before that time came, another church member and I found Jackie dead at his home one Sunday night before a church service. I promised myself I would be at the prayer meetings when they would begin because of Jackie's influence in my life. Those early morning prayer meetings virtually changed my prayer life.

When the three kings come to Elisha, he is angry due to the presence of Jehoram (who has followed the wicked ways of his father, Ahab). The only reason Elisha will help is because of the presence of Jehoshaphat (who generally followed the Lord and was a good king). I doubt I would have been in that prayer meeting had it not been for my association with Jackie. These kings would not have received much-needed water had it not been for their association with Jehoshaphat. In Joseph's story, his brothers would never have come into the blessing of the provision of food during a famine had it not been for their association with him, now that Joseph was second in command to Pharaoh.

There are people in your life, and it is possible that they may come into blessings simply because of their association with you. As God blesses you, those blessings reach out and overflow to others. As you move with God's favour upon you, they are being influenced for good. Who can you influence today?

DAY 28

Fading Into The Background

But now bring me a minstrel. And it came to pass, when the minstrel played, that the hand of the LORD came upon him.
2nd Kings 3:15

Outside most churches is a noticeboard on which you can find out what days the various services occur. You can also discover the name of the minister of the church. Don't be distracted by that person's name being highlighted. Just as important are the unsung servants of that particular church who tirelessly work in its various ministries and behind the scenes.

Later in the story, we will read about an amazing miracle which takes place. But there is a character in the story who is usually forgotten about. Before Elisha does anything, he calls for a minstrel (or a harpist). This musician plays some music, and while doing so, God moves in power on Elisha. We never hear of that particular harpist again as they completely exit the story.

That is the mark of a faithful servant of God. It's not about them, but it's all about the Lord. John the Baptist said Jesus must increase, and he must decrease (John 3:30). If you like, John was the *warm-up act* before *the leading player* (Jesus), and once He took centre stage, John got out of the way. As the crowds thronged to Jordan during a mighty revival of repentance, John took all attention away from himself and proclaimed, *'Behold the Lamb of God, Which takes away the sin of the world'* (John 1:29).

There are times when God moves in a service, and souls are saved. Often, it has been due to the Spirit of God moving as the worship team has led the congregation into the presence of God. The worship team fades into the background. Maybe a child comes to Jesus during a *kid's talk*, but earlier, someone had read a simple Bible story which spoke to the child. The helper simply faded into the background. The joy for a true servant comes not in receiving credit but in being used for the Kingdom, getting out of the way, and letting God have all the glory. Is that enough for us?

DAY 29

The Peace That Praise Brings

But now bring me a minstrel. And it came to pass, when the minstrel played, that the hand of the LORD came upon him.
2nd Kings 3:15

Two friends of ours went most Friday evenings into Belfast with clothing and other essentials for people experiencing homelessness. It was something they felt the Lord had put on their hearts. I went along with them one evening to see them at work. We eventually came to a shop entrance as they interacted with various people. The shop was closed as it was late evening, and two or three people were gathered there for shelter. One of the men began to curse and swear at us for no reason. Out of the blue, someone from our group began to sing, *'Jesus loves me, this I know.'*[6] The aggressive spirit in that man immediately disappeared. He went completely quiet, and if I remember correctly, there were tears in his eyes. The sudden transformation in his spirit was remarkable. This incident reminds me of David, who played his harp for King Saul when he was being tormented. The music brought peace to the troubled king. Music is undoubtedly a powerful tool which can be used for good or evil.

It seems that Elisha has become a bit agitated at the presence of Jehoram, and he may have called this harpist to bring calm to his mind as he enquired of God. But there seems to be something more. There was some sort of anointing over the music as the power of God fell on Elisha. There is nothing like music and singing which has been anointed. You can experience this on your own or fellowshipping with other believers. Ephesians 5:19 encourages us to sing and make music in our hearts to the Lord. Over and over, the message of the Psalms is, *'Praise the Lord.'* When we praise the Lord, the Spirit of God can take those words (and even the music) and bring calm and peace to our souls. It's not always easy. You may have to praise until you break down a mental or emotional barrier. But that breakthrough is worthwhile as you feel the power of God flow over your soul. Praise works.

DAY 30

Picking Up The Shovel

And he said, Thus says the LORD, Make this valley full of ditches.
For thus says the LORD, You shall not see wind,
neither shall you see rain; yet that valley shall be filled with water,
that you may drink, both you, and your cattle, and your beasts.
2nd Kings 3:16,17

A missionary is crying to God about a financial need. The following day, the exact money required comes through a bank transfer. God could have miraculously made cash appear before their very eyes. Still, He chose to use a human being to send the money. God doesn't need to use people for anything at all. He just has to speak the Word (as in creation), and it is done. But He chooses ordinary people like you and me.

The Lord instructs Elisha to tell the kings and their armies that they have to make the valley full of ditches. No wind will blow, no rain will come, and God will fill the valley with the water they needed so much at that time. God will perform a miracle, but they will have to participate in that miracle. Could God have made ditches appear? Yes. But He wanted them to do the digging. Something similar takes place at the *Wedding of Cana* (John 2). Could Jesus have just made wine appear in the empty vessels? Of course. But the servants had to fill the pots with water and then pour them out. They had to participate. Why?

Instructing someone to dig a ditch (when there is no prospect at all of any water) will take faith. God does it to test their faith. As that person steps out in faith and begins to dig, it creates within them a spirit of anticipation and expectation as to what God is going to do. While digging ditches, there will no doubt be obstacles and problems along the way. Overcoming these obstacles helps to strengthen faith. Finally, when the job is done, there is that sense of partnership in working with God, which again builds up faith. Are you being asked to dig a ditch today? Are you being asked to partner with God as He works in people's lives? What a privilege it is. Pick up that shovel and *go through with God.*

DAY 31

Putting The Shovel Into The Ground

And he said, Thus says the LORD, Make this valley full of ditches.
2nd Kings 3:16a

Sam has a great children's ministry. He travels Northern Ireland (and even across the world) with puppets and various other forms of entertainment to bring the gospel in a novel and exciting way to kids. I will never forget the night he was at our church, throwing three sharp scythes in the air (at the same time) and catching them by the handle. I had visions of blood all over the carpet, but all went well. It is almost like second nature to him (it would need to be!). What he does takes a lot of skill and faith. But I wonder who was the first person to ever pick up a scythe (or something sharp) and think it was a good idea to juggle and try to catch it? That took even more faith because they had never seen anyone else do it before.

Moses stood at the Red Sea and looked at the impossible. No human in history had ever parted a sea in two and walked across it as if on dry land. Moses trusted God, stretched out his hand, and the waters opened. No one had ever dug ditches in a dry place to be supernaturally filled with water (without a rain cloud in sight). They were participating in the impossible. Just as I wonder who was the first person to attempt to juggle knives, I wonder who was the first to strike the ground that day with their shovel. That was a step of faith, and then the others followed their lead.

Digging spiritual ditches is the preparation work carried out in anticipation of something we are believing that God will do, and that first step of faith is so important. It may be a step into the unknown. Maybe there are those who tell you it has never been done before. They inform you that you have lost your mind. To be fair, digging ditches and expecting rain from nowhere is indeed a crazy thing, unless God tells you to do so. If you are sure that you have heard from God (no matter how crazy the thing seems), take that first step. Put your shovel in the ground. And leave God to do his part and provide the rain.

DAY 32

Keep The Vision Alive

And he said, Thus says the LORD, Make this valley full of ditches.
2nd Kings 3:16a

I told you about the large hedge my grandmother insisted had to be cut with hedge clippers rather than electric ones. It was an all-day job. As I stood there at the start of the day and looked at the task ahead, it seemed it would take forever. But once I began to pace myself, taking it section by section and keeping the final goal in view, it all came together, and I got the job done. I suppose you could call it *playing the long game.*

Can you imagine how this army felt as Elisha told them of the task ahead? They had already been travelling for seven days and had run out of water. They were no doubt tired and perhaps even dehydrated. Surely, it was time to sit back and see the salvation of the Lord! They *would* eventually, but first, they had to start digging. It must have seemed like an impossible task to weary soldiers. I wonder how they kept themselves motivated? I think it was the prospect of what was ahead. God had promised that if they would dig, He would fill the ditches with water. Faith, I believe, motivated tired men to keep digging. It kept the vision alive.

As we seek to *go through with God* and carry out whatever He has given us to do, it is possible to get tired. Even Jesus became physically weary as He sat on Sychar's well (John 4:6). Jesus recognised our need for rest and encouraged the disciples to come aside and rest in a quiet place (Mark 6:31). But (assuming we are putting aside the necessary time to recharge our physical, emotional and spiritual batteries), how do we cope with the general weariness that can come as we grind away daily, trying to do our best for the Lord? God's part is that He gives us the strength and the power through His Spirit (Zechariah 4:6). Our part, I believe, is to *play the long game* and by faith, keep the vision alive. What is the vision? Souls saved? Lives restored? Communities changed? Prodigals coming home? Keep your eye on the end goal. Believe in the promises of God. Don't give up. Keep digging.

DAY 33

Doing The Spadework

And he said, Thus says the LORD, Make this valley full of ditches.
2nd Kings 3:16a

When your pastor preaches a thirty-minute sermon, it doesn't mean he took just thirty minutes to prepare it. It's just the same as when you get a meal made for you. Just because you eat it in twenty minutes doesn't mean it took twenty minutes to prepare! As you gaze in wonder at that beautiful art on a plate in front of you, the kitchen will look completely different. You will find peeled skins from vegetables, discarded parts of meat and bones, experiments gone wrong (that's the worrying part), dirty spoons, ladles, knives, bowls, plates and saucepans. You are only presented with the final result of perhaps hours of work. Similarly, your pastor presents the result of hours of laborious study and spadework in those thirty minutes.

The end result of our passage sees empty ditches miraculously filled with water. Before that could happen, there were possibly hours of tough spadework as the soldiers dug those ditches. *Going through with God* requires some spadework. Digging spiritual ditches in anticipation of God filling them requires some spadework. Let me again emphasise that God gives according to His grace and not based on our '*performance*'. We don't work *for* the blessing, but work in partnership *with God* as He moves in our hearts and *freely pours out the blessing.*

Jesus described some of the needed spadework by encouraging us to ask, seek and knock. The meaning in the original language in Luke 11:9 is to ask (and keep on asking), seek (and keep on seeking), knock (and keep on knocking). Hosea 10:12 says to break up the unploughed ground of our hearts. As we allow that shovel to dig deep in our hearts, Hosea indicates it should lead us to seek the Lord. The end result will see His rain of righteousness being poured out upon us. The spadework can be challenging, and it may seem like nothing is happening. Look to God and keep digging. He gives the increase (1st Corinthians 3:6).

DAY 34

Are You Desperate Enough To Dig?

And he said, Thus says the LORD, Make this valley full of ditches.
2nd Kings 3:16a

As a church, we recently completed a six-week project called, *'Digging Ditches For Donaghcloney.'* Those who took part in the project were given the name of someone who needed prayer for health or else salvation. Each person would commit to praying daily for that name and (if medically feasible) fast one meal a week. Other needs were also included in the general prayers. It took some discipline and was a hard grind, but I believe there was a spirit of unity and teamwork. We hope to take this up again in the near future. We do not know when, how or in what way God will respond, but we have done our part in digging the ditches, and we believe that He can fill them as and when He pleases.

Who can you dig a ditch for and look to God to fill it with water? Perhaps it is an unsaved friend or a prodigal. It could be someone who is sick. Do you need to dig a ditch for your marriage? What about your family? I'm sure your local church has plenty of ditches which need digging. Who is going to take up a spade? Who will plunge it into the ground even though the situation seems impossible? As you break up that ground, others may be encouraged to do the same. As the sweat drops fall from your head, as you keep digging (despite no rain clouds) and break through the pain barrier of weariness, others may be inspired to step out in faith, too.

Our world today is crying out for people who will discipline themselves, resolve to dig those ditches and reach out in faith to God. If we don't do it, who will? We saw how desperate these men were for water. Is anyone desperate enough to start digging? Has anyone reached the stage, like these men, where there's nothing left to do but stare the impossible in the face, start digging and dare to believe God can do the filling? There's nothing to lose and so much to gain. Be encouraged. Pick up that shovel and get digging.

DAY 35

Diligent Faith Digs Deep

And this is but a light thing in the sight of the LORD:
He will deliver the Moabites also into your hand.
2nd Kings 3:18

The events at Dunkirk in 1940 were miraculous. The Allied soldiers must have felt like the Israelites trapped at the Red Sea (except there was no Moses to part the waters). It seemed that all would be lost. However, King George VI called for Sunday, 26th May 1940, to be observed as a *National Day of Prayer*. The nation responded to his call, as did millions across the Commonwealth and British Empire. Ditches were being dug, and soon, God would respond and fill them. In his book, *'The Trumpet Sounds For Britain,'* David E. Garder tells of three miracles that took place.[7] For some reason, Hitler halted the advance of his armoured columns, which were only ten miles away from reaching the Allied troops. Then, an unexpected storm prevented the Luftwaffe from doing untold damage. Lastly, a great calm settled over the English Channel, greatly aiding the flotilla of ships sent to help with the evacuation. Around 300,000 soldiers were rescued. Churchill had only expected that figure to be 20,000 to 30,000.

God responded to a nation at prayer but did so in a way that was beyond its expectations. Something similar happens here. The three kings and their armies faced defeat, having run out of water. God will fill ditches with water if they do their part and dig them. But we are told here that this is just a small thing in God's eyes. He will do a greater miracle and give them victory over the enemy. God far exceeded their expectations.

As you do the preparation work and dig ditches in expectation for God to fill them, widen the horizons of your faith. You may have in your mind what you think God may do, but leave room for Him to do so much more. Hebrews 11:6 reminds us that God loves faith. In fact, He rewards those who diligently (or earnestly) seek Him. *Diligent faith digs deep.* The deeper you dig your ditches, the greater is your expectation that God can fill them.

DAY 36

Dig Out The Dirt, Then Fill With Water

And it came to pass in the morning, when the meat offering was offered,
that, behold, there came water by the way of Edom,
and the country was filled with water.
2nd Kings 3:20

'C*ome on, girls, eat your dinner.' 'We aren't hungry.'* Then you find out they aren't hungry as they have been eating snacks since coming home from school. It's hard to fill a stomach with a good meal when it is already full of rubbish! Our passage shows that the freshly dug, empty ditches are now *'Filled with water.'* They couldn't have been filled with water if they had still been full of dirt from the ground.

It is good to seek to be filled with God's Spirit, as God desires this for our lives (see Ephesians 5:18). However, some digging may need to be done and some cleansing to remove the dirt from us. A lot of rubbish may need to be emptied in order for the cleansing and flowing power of the Spirit to immerse us. It is the Blood of Jesus that can cleanse us from our sin (1st John 1:7). When we allow this digging and cleansing of our hearts to take place, then we can be set apart and ready for the Lord to use us (2nd Timothy 2:21). Our freshly cleansed vessels can then be filled to overflowing with the Spirit of God.

As we finish this particular section on digging ditches, I want you to notice the beginning of this verse: *'It came to pass.'* Just as God had promised, so it came to pass that the ditches were filled with water. Their faith and diligence were rewarded. Sometimes, our girls ask if they can do a specific thing later in the day, and initially, I may say *'Yes,'* but due to unforeseen circumstances, we have to change plans. They are very disappointed, and I feel bad about it. But when God promises something, you will never be disappointed. None of His promises have failed to date, and they never will. You may have to wait a period of time for them to come to pass, but there is no *use-by-date* on God's Word. Keep waiting and trusting. If He has promised it, He will do it.

SECTION 4

ESSENTIAL OIL

2nd Kings 4:1-7

DAY 37

Run To Jesus

Now there cried a certain woman of the wives of the sons of the prophets unto Elisha, saying,
2nd Kings 4:1a

I don't know if you have noticed it, but in the movies or a TV series, when someone is being chased, they usually find their way into a building and run upwards. The camera follows them as they run up one, two, three and four flights of stairs with those chasing them in hot pursuit. Then they open a door at the top, run through it and find that they are on the rooftop of a multi-story car park. There is nowhere else to go except down (over the side of the roof!) It is a dead end. You would think that by now, those being chased would have seen enough movies to know that!

Where do you go when you are in trouble? Where do you run, and who do you run to? If we don't run to God, we will find that we are hopelessly running up a staircase and onto a flat rooftop with nowhere else to go. And we do it time and time again.

In this story, we read of a woman in big trouble. Her husband has died. In those times, we know that women didn't get the best of deals in life. If the breadwinner (the husband) died, your family would suffer financial hardship. In Bible times, a prophet was seen as a representative of the Lord. This woman cries out to Elisha about her problem. There is no doubt her problem is a *'biggie.'* By calling on Elisha, she is effectively calling upon God.

I think it would be fair enough to say that many people have at least five *'biggie'* problems in their lives. A personal, private problem that you generally keep to yourself. A family problem. A work-associated problem. A health problem. A financial problem. Whatever your problem is, have you called upon the Lord? The woman did well to run to Elisha. However, the amazing thing is that you, as a Blood-bought, redeemed child of God, have direct access to your High Priest, Jesus, Who sits upon the throne of grace. He is touched by the things you are going through. Before you run to anyone else, run to Jesus.

DAY 38

The Question Of Suffering

Your servant my husband is dead; and you know that your servant did fear the LORD: and the creditor is come to take to him my two sons to be bondmen.
2nd Kings 4:1b

One of the greatest questions in the human heart is that of suffering. My Dad's brother, Stanley, and his wife, Rachel, had a little boy named Karl, who had leukaemia. One of his great wishes was to ride in a helicopter. The army made his dream come true before he died at the tender age of six. The family moved to Canada in the 1970s, and some years later, Karl's brother Garry died in a tragic farming incident involving a truck. He was only seventeen. Then, in 2013, a third son, Craig, died in a motorcycle accident at the age of forty. This came just a matter of weeks after his Dad (Uncle Stanley) received his Home call. The mind struggles to process this and the grief and questions that come with it. Why should this happen to a Christian family that loves God? For Aunt Rachel and daughter Ingrid and the family, it has only been the grace of God that has carried them through.

This story is about a woman who was married to one of the sons of the prophets. He was a godly man. But he has died. His wife has had to borrow money; she cannot pay it back, and the creditors were going to come to take her sons as servants. Why should this happen to such a God-fearing family?

We may try to answer the suffering question as best we can, but we will never have the perfect answer. Intellectual reasoning can never heal a broken heart. Only a loving God can do that. He binds up the broken-hearted (Psalm 147:3). The language of tears is the same in Australia, Canada, Germany, China, Brazil and Africa. God understands that language. Jesus spoke the language of tears while here on Earth (John 11:35). Today, He is touched by your tears, and in that great tomorrow, He will wipe them all from your eyes (Revelation 21:4). Someday, He will wipe the tears from the eyes of Aunt Rachel and Ingrid too. This is our comfort and hope.

DAY 39

A "Doer"

And Elisha said to her, What shall I do for you?
2nd Kings 4:2a

Some people in life are *'doers.'* They are the sort of people who are there for you in a crisis, roll their sleeves up and help in whatever way they can. Due to Dad's illness from his early thirties, there were many times when he was rushed into hospital very ill. There were certain people who would say to Mum, *'Right, Lorna, what is it that you need done?'* They would have done the washing, errands, or looked after Lynne and me, who were only young at the time (while Mum and Granny dealt with the crisis at hand). To this day, the family still remembers those self-sacrificial gestures of practical kindness gratefully.

Elisha is a *'doer.'* The woman comes to him with her troubles, and he says, in effect, *'OK. Tell me what it is that you need done.'* Elisha's title may be that of a prophet, but he is also a servant. As a Christian, you may be known to others as a teacher, factory worker, homemaker, pastor or shop assistant, but you can add the title of *servant.* Elisha was a *'doer'* for the Kingdom of God in his walk of life. Wherever your sphere of influence is in life, it goes hand in hand with being a servant of the Kingdom of God. It is great to sit in church and learn the great truths of the Bible (and vital if we are to mature in our walk with God), but hearing is not enough. James 1:22 says we are to be *'doers'* and not only hearers. And *doing* in the Bible involves *serving.*

We will meet various people along the road of life today. Each one will have different types of needs. If someone expresses a need to you today, why not ask them, '*What is it that I can do to help?'* But here is a greater challenge: pray about it first, and then come alongside someone today who hasn't even expressed any need to you at all and say, *'I have been praying and was wondering, is there anything I can do for you?'* Even if they answer, *'No thanks,'* you have shown them that you care, and you may have an opportunity in the future to serve them. Be a *'doer.'*

DAY 40

What Have <u>You</u> Got?

.....tell me, what have you in the house? And she said, Your handmaid has not any thing in the house, save a pot of oil.
2nd Kings 4:2b

Something had gone wrong with the mechanism in the handle of our bedroom window, and it would not close properly. A friend, Jim, looked at it and realised that a new mechanism was required, as it had snapped. But until it could be ordered, we would need something temporary to keep the window closed and keep the heat in. Jim asked if we had a metal tube and string in the house. We didn't (imagine having no string!) but found a piece of an extension for a window-cleaning brush, along with some plastic cable ties. That is what held our window together. Anyone looking from the outside may have thought we had lost the plot! Jim improvised, using what we had in the house.

Something similar happens here. The woman asks Elisha for help. He has said he will help. But he turns it back to her: what have <u>*you*</u> got in the house? When the disciples came to Jesus, panicking because of a large crowd that needed to be fed, He said, *'<u>You</u> give them to eat'* and then asked how many loaves they had (Mark 6:37-38). Jesus used the little food they had to feed the multitude. When Moses doubted his ability to lead God's people, the Lord asked, *'What is that in <u>your</u> hand?'* (Exodus 4:2). God used what Moses had to accomplish the job. The lesson is this: bring what little you have to the Lord, and He can use it for His glory. What use were five loaves and two fish? It was plenty for God. What use was a rod against the might of Egypt? It was enough for God.

You will notice that when Elisha first asked what she had, the woman replied that she had *nothing*. But then, almost as an afterthought, she mentioned the pot of oil. It was her afterthought (the thing which she deemed most insignificant) that was used for a miracle. Maybe you think you have nothing to offer God in the way of gifting. You believe what you have is insignificant. Just dedicate it to the Lord. You will be surprised by what He can do.

DAY 41

Great Expectations

Then he said, Go, borrow you vessels abroad of all your neighbours, even empty vessels; borrow not a few.
2nd Kings 4:3

When you come to church, what are your expectations? Do you expect things just to be much the same as the previous week, or do you anticipate God moving in a fresh way? When reading the Bible, do you just read it like you would read a storybook, or are you expecting to meet with God as you read its pages? When you pray, do you expect to leave the place of prayer rejuvenated and refreshed, or do you think you will be just the same as when you started to pray? If we believe God is a mighty, powerful God Who refreshes and pours out blessings, gives us strength for the day, and fills us with His Spirit, then surely, we should be people of *great expectations*.

Elisha has asked this lady what she has in the house. She replies that she has only a pot of oil. He tells her to go to her neighbours and borrow empty vessels (or jars). *'Oh, and while you are there, make sure it's not just a few jars. You are going to need a lot.'* At this stage, I would be asking questions. '*What are you going to do with a load of empty jars? Surely you aren't going to fill them with the little oil that I have?'* If you read the rest of the verses, you will notice that this lady never once raises a complaint or a protest at what she is being asked to do. This is a prophet from God, and she is going to believe what he tells her. What amazing faith she had.

This lady not only had faith but also *great expectations*. The extent of this miracle (as we will see) depends on how many jars she brings home. If she didn't have *great expectations* and wasn't sure if this would work, she might have just asked for one or two jars and kept it low-key. But if she really trusts and expects God to move, she will do as the prophet asks and borrow many. In the rest of the story, she obeys Elisha one hundred per cent, so we assume here she also obeyed and brought many jars back. Are you *expecting great things* from God today?

DAY 42

Shut Out

And when you are come in, you shall shut the door upon you and upon your sons.....
2nd Kings 4:4a

Is the glass half full, or is it half empty? Is it partly sunny or partly cloudy outside? When you close a door, is it to shut someone in or to shut someone out? Today, we read about a shut door. The woman has borrowed jars from her neighbours. She is told to close the door and then follow more instructions. But why has she to shut the door? Initially, the idea seems to be to shut the woman and her son inside (we will look at that tomorrow). But was it also to shut some people out?

In the story of Jairus' daughter in Mark chapter 5, when Jesus said that the girl was sleeping (to Jesus, raising the dead was like waking someone out of sleep), they laughed at Him. So, Jesus put them all out! Without faith, it is impossible to please God. A great miracle was about to take place, so Jesus put the doubters and the mockers out. God operates in an atmosphere of faith.

How would this relate to our story? Mum had a neighbour who admitted to being nosey. She used to tell Mum what time her lights had been switched off the previous night! (Mum lived in a corner house). Our neighbour used to joke that she was envious of Mum because she could see everything going on from the top and bottom sides of the street, whereas she could only see up one side.

Here's my point: nosey neighbours. This woman had borrowed a lot of jars from her neighbours. Would they have crowded around the house, curious about what was happening? Do you think some of them may have been sceptical and put some doubts in the woman's head? It doesn't say, but I think Elisha wanted the door shut to keep nosey doubters out. If you want to *go through with God,* there will be those who will try and dampen your enthusiasm and speak doubts into your situation. Make sure you have a close circle of faith-filled friends. Faith feeds faith and builds it up. Shut the door on doubt, and believe in God for great things.

DAY 43

Shut In

And when you are come in, you shall shut the door upon you and upon your sons, and shall pour out into all those vessels, and you shall set aside that which is full.
2nd Kings 4:4

Yesterday, we saw a shut door and looked at the possibility that it may have been closed in order to keep doubters out. However, the text indicates it was closed, so the mother and her two sons would be shut inside. Elisha will have all three participate in this miracle rather than sit as spectators. He would give them the opportunity to experience the power of God for themselves. Imagine what might have happened if Elisha had just performed this miracle himself. It would have been amazing, but they wouldn't have had this personal experience for themselves. For this miracle to happen, they had to obey Elisha's instructions and simultaneously exercise their faith in God. They needed this time alone with God and to have no other distractions.

It is great to fellowship with other Christians and experience God's power and presence together, but we must also have moments alone with Him. We need to be shut in with God and shut everything else out. We can only build intimacy with God when we personally experience His presence. It is good to read books about how others have experienced the power of God, but just reading about it falls short of the reality. We need to experience God for ourselves.

In Luke 6:12, we read that Jesus went up a mountain and continued all night in prayer to God. Jesus shut Himself in with His Father. We never read what he prayed that night. It was something for just Jesus and His Father to experience.

Elisha told this woman that she had to shut the door. It was something she had to do for herself. It is something we have to do, too. It is a decision we have to make. Will we shut out the distractions and shut ourselves in with God?

DAY 44

Precious Instructions

So she went from him, and shut the door upon her and upon her sons, who brought the vessels to her; and she poured out.
2nd Kings 4:5

Do you ever struggle with instructions? In our house, any self-assembled projects usually end up with Di figuring them out. When a new gadget (perhaps a mobile phone) is bought, I prefer to play around with it and find out how it works rather than read the manual. It's more fun that way! I struggle when asking directions, especially when I hear instructions like this: *'Go to the end of the road, and you will see a house with an orange door. You can't miss it. It stands out a mile. You know the one I'm talking about? Well, when you come to it, just ignore it and keep on going. After two, well, maybe five minutes, depending on how fast you drive, you will go through one, two, or three traffic lights. No, actually, it's only two……'* The confusion continues, and I end up wishing I had never asked!

Elisha gave this woman a set of instructions, and she followed each one to the very letter, regardless of how impossible it seemed. She only had a tiny amount of oil, yet she was expected to keep pouring into all the jars. How could this be possible? She never questioned but kept pouring. *Going through with God* (for her) meant battling against impossibilities and unconditional obedience.

We can mistake instructions as being a nuisance. In the Christian life, we often emphasise that we do not live a legalistic life of *'do's and don'ts'* as we now live in the liberty of Jesus. But that does not give us a license to do whatever we please. The instructions God has given us do not save us (we are saved through faith in Christ alone), but those who follow them make a wise choice. We don't obey in a robotic, legalistic way but with a heart that has been won by Jesus' love for us at Calvary. The Psalmist said that he loved God's commandments more than gold (Psalm 119:127). That means he saw them as *precious* rather than a *nuisance.* What value do we put on His instructions?

DAY 45

According To Your Faith

And it came to pass, when the vessels were full, that she said to her son,
Bring me yet a vessel. And he said to her,
There is not a vessel more. And the oil stayed.
2nd Kings 4:6

There used to be a restaurant nearby which was especially good for kids (small and big!) You would be entitled to unlimited ice cream and soft drinks when you chose a particular offer. This sounds amazing, and kids imagine that they will eat bowls and bowls of ice cream. However, after the main meal, they begin to feel full, and perhaps only one bowl or two of ice cream is enough. It's not that the unlimited ice cream has run out, but they have nowhere to put it!

The miracle in this story is such that, as long as the woman provides jars, the oil will keep coming. It is an unlimited supply. The oil will stop only when there is nowhere left to put it.

This teaches us something about faith. If the woman had only brought back one or two jars from her neighbours, she would only have filled one or two. If she had brought back ten or fifteen, she would have filled ten or fifteen. The measure of her faith would determine how much oil she would have. Imagine if Noah had only the faith to build a small boat. It wouldn`t have been enough to carry the mass of animals he would have to bring. But he followed God's instructions and had the faith to build the ark.

Whatever you have faith to believe for, then that is the extent of what you can really hope for. If you can stretch your faith to believe for more, then subsequently, you can expect more. How far your faith extends depends on how big you believe your God is. Limiting God may limit the outcome of whatever you are believing Him to do. Having said that, God often surprises us, even though our faith has been small. Paul reminds us we have a God Who is able to do far more than we can even ask or think (Ephesians 3:20). Although the final result is according to His Will, it is better to reach out and stretch our faith rather than have low expectations.

DAY 46

Unlimited Resources

Then she came and told the man of God. And he said, Go, sell the oil, and pay your debt, and live you and your children of the rest.
2nd Kings 4:7

Without going into the details, we once received a bill for a large enough sum of money due to an error on someone else's part. At that time, I was attending Bible College four days a week, and we were watching our finances. We appealed the bill three times and brought the matter to the Lord. But on receiving the third correspondence, we were informed that although the error was not our fault, the money was still owed and needed to be paid. It was disappointing, and we resigned ourselves to paying the money. On the same day that we received the final correspondence, I was contacted by two people who said that the Lord had put it on their hearts to send us a gift. We had not told anyone about this financial situation. The two gifts together paid the bill and left money to spare. God gave us more than we even needed.

We saw that the oil filled all the jars the woman borrowed, and now Elisha tells her to sell it, pay her debt and live off the rest of the money. Paul tells us that God will supply our needs (Philippians 4:19), and on this occasion (as He so often does), He provided over and above their needs. Paul adds that the Lord supplies our needs 'According to His riches in glory by Christ Jesus.' Yesterday, we saw we can expect to receive from God according to (in proportion to) our faith. Today, we see we can expect to have our needs met in proportion to His riches in Jesus.

God is a God of unlimited resources. He overflows with blessings and grace. When God saved us, He didn't just do exactly what was required to the letter of the law and leave it there. Like Mephibosheth, we, who were *'dead dogs,'* now eat continually at the king's table (2nd Samuel 9:7,8). Through what Jesus did on the cross, His unmerited and amazing grace has brought us into blessings that will last through all eternity. What a Saviour.

SECTION 5

FAITH AND STRUGGLES

2nd Kings 4:8-37

DAY 47

Perceiving Others' Needs

And it fell on a day, that Elisha passed to Shunem, where was a great woman; and she constrained him to eat bread. And so it was, that as often as he passed by, he turned in there to eat bread.
2nd Kings 4:8

The floor is littered with toys and looks like a war zone. You scan your eyes around the room and observe one child lying on the sofa (giggling while she watches TV) while the other sits among the mess, calmly eating a packet of crisps. Both are blissfully unaware of the chaos they have created around them. They don't recognise any need to tidy up. Can someone please reassure me that this state of mind changes as they get older?

The story we begin today is usually called *'The Shunammite Woman'* (as she comes from a place called Shunem). She is described as a *'great'* woman, which speaks of her wealth, but we find throughout the story that she is also great in character.[8] Elisha travelled extensively, and of course, there were no fast-food outlets to stop at. One day, this woman saw Elisha on his travels and gave him some food to eat. From that time onwards, he stopped there to eat whenever he passed that way. Unlike my kids (who were totally unaware of the need to tidy the room), the Shunammite woman was very aware of Elisha's need for food. Not only that, but she did something about his requirements and helped him.

As Christians, we should be aware of the needs of others around us. We follow Jesus, Who saw the necessities of others when no one else was aware at all. Paul instructs us in Philippians 2:4 not to look at our own interests but at the interests of others. How easy it is to get wrapped up in our own little world.

To recognise the needs of those around us will require a heart of compassion. A caring person looks a little deeper at a situation and sees requirements that aren't necessarily obvious to others. We also should be in touch with the Lord. Often, it is the prompting of the Holy Spirit Who moves us to help someone. We will encounter people with needs today. May God help us to perceive those needs.

DAY 48

A Heart Overflowing With Kindness

Let us make a little chamber, I pray you, on the wall; and let us set for him there a bed, and a table, and a stool, and a candlestick: and it shall be, when he comes to us, that he shall turn in there.
2nd Kings 4:10

Auntie Mamie (Mum's cousin) passed away recently. Neither had any siblings and treated each other as sisters. I had the privilege of reading a tribute at the funeral (which was written by her daughter, Jacqueline). As we considered Auntie Mamie's life, a theme of hospitality became clear. The family home was opened to welcome evacuees during the *Second World War.* A few years later, Mum's father died (when she was only twelve), and the house was opened for her and Granny to stay for around a year. In 2017, after extensive work had to be done to Mum's house, she was welcomed (along with my sister) into Auntie Mamie's home for over four months. We will never forget her kindness, and she is greatly missed.

The Shunammite woman suggests to her husband that they not only feed Elisha, but prepare somewhere for him to sleep if he needs to rest as he travels around. Here, we see this woman going way above and beyond the call of duty. She doesn't have to do this, but she does. Why? Because she perceives that Elisha is a *man of God* (see verse 9). It is because of Whom Elisha serves. She is doing it for the sake not only of Elisha but of the Lord. This woman's heart is overflowing with kindness. How much more should ours, as Blood-bought sons and daughters of God? Surely, we can go above and beyond the call of duty because Jesus did the same for us when He left Heaven to die for our sins.

What can we provide for someone today, for Jesus' sake? How can we show the love and grace of God to others? Don't just give to them according to the letter of the law, but go beyond their expectations, go the extra mile and lavish kindness on them. *The extraordinary love of Jesus should transform us into people with extraordinary hearts of love for others.*

. DAY 49

Don't Give Up Praying

And he said, What then is to be done for her? And Gehazi answered, Verily she has no child, and her husband is old.
2nd Kings 4:14

Dad prayed most of his life for the salvation of one of his brothers but never lived to see his prayers answered. However, Uncle Harry got saved around six months after Dad's Home call to Heaven. About six months later, Uncle Harry also passed away. Waiting for prayers to be answered is the hard part. We are prone to give up if we have been praying for something for ten, twenty or thirty years (or more).

In Bible times, a great desire of parents was to have children, but more importantly, a son. This would mean a continuation of the family name and someone to look after everything if the father died. We learn in this passage that the Shunammite woman has no children and her husband is now old. Her hopes and dreams of a son had probably been buried in her heart many years previously.

Elisha is so grateful for her kindness and (through his servant, Gehazi) asks what he can do for her. She says she is content. Gehazi, however, points out that she has no children. Elisha calls her over and says that she will have a child. This hits a raw nerve. It seems to be a hurt that is hidden in her heart. She pleads with Elisha not to lie to her about such a thing. But Elisha wasn`t lying.

It seems a logical conclusion that the more the years pass by, the less likely it is that our prayers will be answered. But this is not always the case. Although it is true that sometimes the answer to our prayers is *'No,'* yet at other times, it is *'Wait.'* Caleb received a promise from God that he would enter the Promised Land. It took over forty years for that to happen, and it wasn't his fault. He was held back due to the sins of other people. You can see from this that prayers can even be delayed for any number of reasons. But Caleb held on and received the promise. Don't give up. *Go through with God,* and keep holding on in prayer.

DAY 50

Waiting.....

And the woman conceived, and bore a son at that season that Elisha had said to her, according to the time of life.
2nd Kings 4:17

Waiting for a baby's birth can be a happy yet anxious time. Our first child, Ellie, is very easygoing and takes her time. Sure enough, she was several days overdue. On the other hand, Karis, who likes things done *yesterday*, was a few days early. She didn't have time to hang around! I remember the night that it seemed Karis was on the way. We rushed to the hospital, hoping that this was the moment for which we had been waiting. But then we heard the staff talking as if they would send us home again. They went out of the room for a while, and we waited. The funny thing was that I couldn't get a chorus out of my head called *'The move is on!'*[9] I began humming and singing it under my breath while waiting. The staff came back and said they were keeping Di in the hospital. *The move was indeed on*, and soon after, our second little bundle of joy appeared.

It is not only challenging to wait for a baby to be born, but as we saw yesterday, waiting on God can really test us. The Shunammite woman's dreams of having a child were so far gone that she pleaded with Elisha not to lie to her. It was a hurtful subject. However, the child was born '*at that season,*' as Elisha had said.

Ecclesiastes chapter 3 reminds us that there are times and seasons for everything. The most crucial calendar is God's calendar. At the appointed time, God sent His Son into the world (Galatians 4:4). He has established the day when He will judge the world (Acts 17:31). We cannot speed up God's clock nor slow it down. His promises will come to pass, but only when He says so.

What do we do in the meantime? Isaiah 40:31 says that waiting on the Lord renews our strength. Psalm 27:14 tells us that waiting on God strengthens our hearts. And just in case we missed the point, David emphasizes a second time: *'Wait, I say, on the Lord.'* There's our answer.

DAY 51

Is It Well?

Run now, I pray you, to meet her, and say to her, Is it well with you? is it well with your husband? is it well with the child?
2nd Kings 4:26a

Some of Elisha's miracles involve very raw and devastating circumstances. We have already seen a woman whose godly husband has died, and her sons are about to be taken away as slaves. In the story of the Shunammite woman, there is a tragic twist. Having shown considerable hospitality to Elisha, she has been miraculously granted the birth of a son. But we are not prepared for what happens next. The boy, having grown up, suddenly dies. Next, we will see the human struggle between faith and untold grief.

Before we look at her struggles, I want to consider the words of today's verse. The woman lays her son in Elisha's room (the prophet is not there) and makes her way as quickly as possible to find him. As Elisha sees her approaching, he tells his servant Gehazi to ask her if everything is well with herself and her family.

Horatio Spafford wrote the famous hymn, 'It is well with my soul,'[10] and I want to take Elisha's question and simply ask it to you as you read this book. Is it well with your soul? Do you know Jesus Christ as your personal Saviour? The sole reason Horatio Spafford could make it through life, having lost four of his daughters in a tragic sea accident, was knowing that all was well with his soul. Peace comes through sins forgiven. When all falls around you, it is possible to have the peace of God within you. Paul describes it as a peace that passes all understanding, which guards our minds and hearts (Philippians 4:7).

Is it well with you? Maybe you *are* saved today but are having great trials. Just as Elisha was concerned with the welfare of this woman, the Lord is concerned with your welfare today. He cares for the little sparrow that falls, and He cares for you too. You are invited to cast your care on Jesus today (1st Peter 5:7). Come to Him in your weariness, and He will give you rest (Matthew 11:28).

DAY 52

Single-Mindedness

And she answered, It is well:
2nd Kings 4:26b

'*How are you doing today?' 'Ack, not too bad, thanks.'* Yet inside, your heart is breaking. At some stage, we have all attempted to show a *stiff upper lip.* Retired pastor, Sydney Kerr (who pastored Donaghcloney Elim for many years) has a more realistic answer to this question. When I ask, *'How are you today?'* a little smile comes to his face, and he answers, '*Struggling, but surviving!'* And we have a bit of a laugh. But it is true for most of us, isn't it? We are all struggling, but by God's grace, we are making it through.

When asked how she is doing, the Shunammite woman gives a strange answer: *'It is well.'* How can she say that when things most certainly are not well? Her son has just died while on her lap. I think it is evident that she had come to find Elisha in the hope that he could do something about this situation. Therefore, her answer was an answer of faith. You see, Elijah had previously raised the son of the widow of Zarephath from the dead. By saying, *'It is well,'* it seems she believed by faith that all would indeed be well and that God could use His prophet to raise her son also.

This woman is on a mission and is *going through with God*, no matter what. We read of her single-mindedness in verse 22 as she says that she will rush to Elisha, and significantly she adds, *'And come again.'* She doesn't have failure on her mind. In verse 24, she instructs her servant to hurry and not slack off. If you want to *go through with God*, you will have a single-mindedness about it, and will seek to keep pressing in and pressing on, come what may.

Please understand that God's Spirit is within us, and we don't need to *'chase'* God, as such. He is always there and never leaves us. But we do need to put Him first in our lives. We do need to hunger and thirst for more of Himself. We do require single-mindedness to press on and press in despite the distractions around us. We cannot do this on our own. The Holy Spirit is here to help us.

DAY 53

Keep Holding On

And when she came to the man of God to the hill,
she caught him by the feet:
2nd Kings 4:27a

As I made my way up the driveway of a house, I spied a little terrier dog running my way. It sank its sharp teeth into my ankle and refused to let go. I walked up the driveway that day like someone with a limp. I don't seem to have great experiences with animals or people grabbing my feet. Now and again, as I try to rush out the door, the girls will hold my feet and won't let go. As I limp up the hallway with them both in tow, they scream with laughter as I lift my foot, and they are dragged along the floor. They seem to think it is fun!

The dog and the girls grabbed my feet out of playfulness. Here, the Shunammite woman grabs hold of Elisha's feet, but she is in dead earnest. The indication is that she is hanging on and will not let go. This action speaks of humility, pleading, and absolute resoluteness in what she is doing. It reminds us of Jacob, who wrestled with a mysterious opponent and determined, *'I will not let you go, except you bless me'* (Genesis 32:26). These characteristics which the Shunammite woman displayed are the marks of a person who is *going through with God.* You come in humility, laying yourself at the feet of Jesus. You come to seek, ask and knock. And you won't let go until you get the blessing.

A man came to Jesus in Mark 10:17. The fact that he ran showed earnestness. His kneeling before Jesus indicated humility. His asking of a vital question suggested he was seeking. This man almost *'made it'* but ultimately went away in sadness because he wasn't willing to give everything up and follow Jesus. He wasn't prepared to hold on until he got the blessing and wouldn't *go through with God.*

Keep holding on, as it were, to the feet of Jesus. As you desire to go deeper with the Lord, as you pray for your prodigal or seek guidance for the future, hold on and determine not to let go.

DAY 54

Pushing People Away

.....but Gehazi came near to push her away.
2nd Kings 4:27b

My wife, Di, is originally from Brazil. I joke with her that Pelé was the second-greatest football player of all time. The best was, of course, George Best from our own Northern Ireland. Our Primary School was full of excitement one particular day in the 1970s as a helicopter hovered above the building and landed on the all-weather sports pitch. George Best emerged from the helicopter to the cheers of the waiting crowd. Many could not believe it as they stood just a short distance from their footballing hero. When celebrities mingle with the public in such a way, it must be a nightmare for their *'minders.'* Often, they have to push people away as they try to protect their clients.

When the Shunammite woman grabbed hold of Elisha's feet, I believe that when his servant Gehazi pushed her away, it was not done with any malice intended but for the safety of his master. It was part of his job to look after Elisha.

My thoughts immediately turned to the well-meaning disciples. As mothers came with their children to Jesus, they took the role of *'minders'* and turned them away. They probably figured that Jesus was too busy for something they deemed to be insignificant. They were actually going to stop Jesus from laying His hands on the children and praying for them. But Jesus rebuked them and said not to hinder them from coming, *'For of such is the Kingdom of Heaven'* (Matthew 19:14). We too can unintentionally push people away from Jesus by our words, actions and attitudes. Most have heard that well-worn negative phrase, *'Well, if that's Christianity, I want nothing to do with it.'* While it is true that we are imperfect and do make mistakes, may this not deter us from making it our daily prayer that others will see Jesus through our lives. A magnet can either attract (pull) or repel (push away). Let us *go through with God*, allowing His Spirit to transform our lives, and may we be granted His favour by attracting others to Jesus.

DAY 55

The Struggles Of Faith

Then she said, Did I desire a son of my lord?
did I not say, Do not deceive me?
2nd Kings 4:28

Finding someone to blame goes way back to the Garden of Eden. Adam blamed his wife, and Eve blamed the serpent. Designating a scapegoat seems the natural thing to do, whether in families, marriages, work or government. We have seen the Shunammite woman move rapidly into a posture of faith, as she seems to believe that the man of God may be able to do the impossible. But now we observe how her humanity and grief are mixed with that faith. You see, when trouble comes, we want to trust God and lean on Him, but there is still that within us which aches inside, and many times cannot understand what is happening. So, we try to find that scapegoat, that person to blame, whether it is someone else, ourselves, or even God.

The Shunammite woman has shown great faith already, but as she continues holding on to the prophet, she now has her moment of humanity. She seems to blame Elisha, making it clear that she hadn't asked for a *'miracle son'* in the first place. It was Elisha who had brought the matter up, not her. In a way, she was right. But on the other hand, no doubt the lad had brought great joy to her life, and it wasn't Elisha's fault that he died.

Elisha doesn't say anything at all to contradict her. In fact, when Gehazi went to push her away, his master said to leave her alone as she was distressed. Notice that he doesn't try to give a theological explanation. In grief, people need understanding, comfort, and even moments of silence instead of (often botched) explanations.

Maybe as you face life's trials, you struggle between faith and raw humanity. The Psalms are full of it. One moment, David may be questioning; the next moment, he is trusting. As the seesaw of your emotion alternates between up and down, the Lord's love for you remains the same. He loves you with an everlasting love (Jeremiah 31:3). He understands your frustrations. He cares for you.

DAY 56

Commitment

And the mother of the child said, As the LORD lives, and as your soul lives, I will not leave you. And he arose, and followed her.
2nd Kings 4:30

One parent looking after two young kids doesn't work. Keeping them both in one place is difficult, especially in a large park. It would help if you had eyes in the back of your head. When the girls were younger, now and again, one of them would go off the radar. It was always on the day when you hadn't put a bright yellow coat on them or something that made them easy to spot among all the other kids. There is an awful sinking feeling in the pit of your stomach when you can't see them. Panic sets in, and included in the hundreds of scenarios that flash across your mind is the one where you are trying to explain to your spouse how it all happened. But there's nothing like that feeling of sheer relief when they turn up, and you can breathe again.

The Shunammite woman isn't going to let Elisha out of her sight for one moment. She says the exact words that Elisha said to Elijah in 2nd Kings 2:2. *'As the LORD lives, and as your soul lives, I will not leave you.'* Why did they both say this? Elisha wanted the blessing, and he followed Elijah like a bloodhound. In the Shunammite woman's case, Elisha (having inherited Elijah's mantle) was her son's only hope. She was not going to miss out.

'As the Lord lives' wasn't a casual statement; they were both making a deep commitment. Psalm 37:5 instructs us to, *'Commit your way to the Lord.'* And *going through with God* will take a commitment on your part. Jesus is the answer to whatever you need in your life. He holds the key to your blessing. Whether it is salvation, forgiveness, healing, power, peace or joy, He is what you need. He is your everything.

Commit to staying close to Jesus. Cling to Him. Don't allow yourself to wander away to other sources for whatever you need. He is the only One Who can truly satisfy.

DAY 57

Raised To Life

And he went up, and lay upon the child, and put his mouth upon his mouth, and his eyes upon his eyes, and his hands upon his hands: and stretched himself upon the child; and the flesh of the child waxed warm.
2nd Kings 4:34

When Elisha arrives at the house, one of the first things he does is to shut the door. Once again, as we saw on *Days 42 and 43*, it was vital to shut out anything that would distract or bring doubt, and it was necessary to be shut in with God. Doubt and unbelief interfere with what faith is reaching out to do. The next thing Elisha does is to pray (see verse 33). Before we undertake to do anything for God, we must pray. This great need which was before Elisha sent him to his knees. If we, as God's people, really see the great need that is around us today, it should surely send us to our knees like Elisha. If a church is going to do anything for God, it must realise that the *prayerhouse* is the *powerhouse*. Praying shows our total reliance upon God. Jesus said that without Him, we can do nothing (John 15:5).

What happens next is a miracle. Elisha lies on the child, puts his mouth on the child's mouth, his eyes on the child's eyes, and his hands on the child's hands. His flesh begins to warm, and he is raised from the dead. This is a spiritual picture of what happens when we are saved. At one time, we were completely dead in sin. A dead body cannot do anything for itself. We could not do anything to save ourselves. If Jesus had not come along, we would have been eternally lost. But Jesus reached out to us in mercy and love. He saved us and gave us new life. Abundant life. Eternal life.

Then, just as Elisha did to the young lad, Jesus touched our mouths. Now we sing praises to His Name and tell others about Jesus. He touched our eyes, which were once blinded, and made us see again. He touched our hands and has given us the power to work for Him. Let us continue using our hands, feet, mouths (and all we have) for His glory. Paul says to present our bodies as a living sacrifice to God (Romans 12:1). It is the least we can do.

DAY 58

It Will Be Worth It All

And he called Gehazi, and said, Call this Shunammite. So he called her. And when she was come in to him, he said, Take up your son.
2nd Kings 4:36

Di's brother, Wellington, came to Northern Ireland for a visit around the time of our wedding. I imagined that bringing him up the *Mourne Mountains* was a good idea for some reason. What was I thinking? Wellington had spent time in the Brazilian army. I can vividly remember that there wasn't one drop of sweat on his face. It looked like a bucket of water had been thrown over my head! Every few moments were punctuated with my words, *'Para, para'* (Portuguese for *'Stop, stop')* as I pleaded for a rest. We eventually made it to the top. I would like to say it was worth it all, but from what I recall, there was mist at the summit, and we couldn`t see much of the view.

For the Shunammite woman, it was definitely worth it all when she heard Elisha's words, *'Take up your son.'* The last few moments had been full of frustration, heartache and sheer determination. Even though everything had been against her, she persevered. She *went through with God.* Even amid her tears, she believed God could do something miraculous through the prophet. *'Take up your son'* were the sweetest words she could hear.

The sweetest words that any Christian can surely hear is when, at the end of the journey, we enter into the presence of Jesus and hear those blessed Words, *'Well done, good and faithful servant.'* All the heartaches of life, the turmoil and the tears will fade away on that day. His Words of welcome will fill our souls with gladness. It will be worth it all.

Hebrews 12:2 reminds us of Jesus, Who, for the joy set before Him, endured the Cross. He looked beyond the pain and suffering He would endure and is now seated at the right hand of God. What an example for us. As we endure the trials of life, as we persevere and *go through with God*, we do so knowing that there is joy ahead, and it will be worth it all one day.

SECTION 6

POISON IN THE POT

2nd Kings 4:38-41

DAY 59

Changed Times

And Elisha came again to Gilgal:
and there was a dearth in the land;
2nd Kings 4:38a

In a seaside town called Portrush (on the north coast of Northern Ireland), there was an amusement arcade called *Barry's.* Every child knew its name was associated with fun. Spending time there (and your parents' money) was the highlight of any visit. Sadly, after almost one hundred years of business, they pulled the shutters down on this kids' paradise. However, to the great delight of many, the business was bought over and resurrected. It has a different name but is still the same place. As I walk around with my kids, it seems I have been transported back in time. The place still lives up to its former name.

Elisha comes to a place named Gilgal. Its name was associated with the location where Israel celebrated the Passover once they had crossed the Red Sea. We aren't sure if Elisha is at the same Gilgal,[11] but whether it is the same or not, the name itself to the Israelites was associated with victory. Unfortunately, the place where Elisha finds himself now does not live up to its great name. It is a place of famine. God had warned in Deuteronomy 28:23 that if His people turned from His ways, they would experience drought in the land. The Northern Kingdom to which Elijah and Elisha had been called had long been worshipping other idols, and now the *chickens were coming home to roost.*

Israel was once a great Kingdom under David, but now things had changed. Yet Elisha's story is of a man who *goes through with God* and sees great things done despite the evil all around. As I look at the United Kingdom and think of the great preachers and times of blessing in the past, to a great extent, there is drought in the land (especially as we see the passing of laws contrary to God's Word). We live in *changing times*, but we have an *unchanging God.* We, too, can rise up like Elisha and stand firm in the darkness, seeing great things done for God's glory, even today.

DAY 60

A Famine Of The Word

.....and there was a dearth in the land;
2nd Kings 4:38b

A man visited a group of Christians in Eastern Europe at the time of persecution behind the *Iron Curtain.* He was amazed by the passion of the believers. The church services would keep going on with no one wanting to leave. Their hunger to worship God was very evident. The man asked an old lady how it was that they were so passionate (while in the West, there seemed to be so much apathy). She looked at him and said, *'In the West, your bellies are full, but your hearts are empty. Here, in the East, our bellies are empty, but our hearts are full.'*

We understand from the Word of God that famine not only has a physical aspect but a spiritual one. Amos 8:11 speaks about a famine of the Word of God in the land. The decline of any nation, church or individual almost certainly originates from a neglect of the Bible. God's Word is a lamp to our feet and a light to our path (Psalm 119:105). To neglect His Word is to open ourselves to darkness. His Word is a sharp sword (Hebrews 4:12) which examines our thoughts and intentions. When we neglect the Bible, we are not allowing God's Word to challenge our hearts. The Bible teaches, reproves, corrects and trains us in righteousness (2nd Timothy 3:16-17). When we neglect the Word of God, we deprive ourselves of a weapon to use against the powers of darkness. As Satan tried to tempt Jesus, He replied with the Word of God each time. Satan had no answer against the authority of God's Word.

We don't neglect our physical bodies. We eat several times a day with a few sneaky snacks in between! I used to have midnight snacks when living at home, but Mum saw the fridge light going on at night from her room! I was caught out! Do we feed our physical body but not our spiritual one? If we were to get a spiritual x-ray of our soul, would it be malnourished?' *'Lord, give us this day our spiritual and our physical bread. Amen.'*

DAY 61

We Need Each Other

.....and the sons of the prophets were sitting before him:
2nd Kings 4:38c

A couple of years ago, some Brazilian friends invited us along to Benone, on the north coast of Northern Ireland. Some were hiring out little huts while others brought tents. We cheated and stayed in accommodation nearby! Saturday was the highlight as the kids were able to spend time with their friends in an outdoor swimming pool, followed by a BBQ in the evening. As it got dark, we gathered around a fire and ate roasted marshmallows. The guitars came out, and we sang Christian songs for quite some time. Good Christian fellowship is hard to beat. As we left that night to go to our accommodation, the rain was absolutely pouring out of the heavens, and the ground underneath the tents was drenched. Did we feel a little guilty? No comment!

Here, we have the sons of the prophets gathered together with Elisha. They are having fellowship. Back in 1st Kings 19, Elijah had been in a place of despair. He had wanted to give up. One of the reasons was that he felt he was fighting on his own. He needed to know others were with him. Ultimately, God told him that seven thousand people had not bowed the knee to Baal and that he wasn't alone. But this episode highlights the need for believers to have fellowship with others of the same faith. We weren't made to do it alone. That's why Hebrews 10:25 instructs us not to forsake the assembling of ourselves together. We need each other, and we need to hear from God together as a family.

We all agree that these are dark and dangerous days. The signs of the times seem to be increasing and point towards that great day of victory. The writer to the Hebrews adds that we should gather together even more as we see the Lord's return approaching. When Jesus comes back, we will spend all eternity with our brothers and sisters. Yet we find it hard to spend time with them on planet Earth! Don't be tempted to slack off in these last days, but *go through with God.* We need each other more than ever.

DAY 62

Sitting At His Feet

.....and the sons of the prophets were sitting before him:
2nd Kings 4:38c

Mary sat at Jesus' feet and learned from the Master (Luke 10:39). Paul was instructed in the law of God as he sat at the feet of Gamaliel (Acts 22:3). One of the greatest wonders of Jesus' early life was as a twelve-year-old when He was found in the temple sitting among the teachers, listening and asking them questions (Luke 2:46). What extraordinary humility from the One Who made all things.

Yesterday, we looked at this verse from the angle of fellowship as the sons of the prophets sat in front of Elisha. Today, we view it from the angle of learning. Although the text doesn't say, it is highly likely that these sons of the prophets had been sitting at Elisha's feet, learning from him (as this would have been the posture of the teacher and student). Elisha would have been their instructor.[12] It is encouraging to note that despite the nation's apostasy, a group of men was hungry for God. The evil of their day did not lessen their enthusiasm. While most fish swim easily with the current, salmon swim against the stream. It is easy to go with popular opinion, but it takes backbone to 'swim' against it. These men have backbone and want to know more about God.

In *going through with God*, you will hunger to *know* more about Him. I am speaking here more about *heart knowledge*. It would be awful to *know* the Bible inside out and yet not really *know* Him. Paul said his desire was *'That I may know Him'* (Philippians 3:10). That word, *know*, speaks of deeply personal knowledge, not simply head knowledge.[13] The person who wants to *go through with God* will also have a teachable spirit. It is one thing to hear but another to allow transformation. Sometimes, it will be painful, as pride screams out and the flesh protests. But for those willing to persevere and allow the Spirit to have His way, the results will bring spiritual blessing and a closer walk with God.

DAY 63

A Feast Or A Famine?

.....and he said to his servant, Set on the great pot, and seethe pottage for the sons of the prophets.
2nd Kings 4:38d

There is nothing like a bowl of homemade *Irish Stew* on a cold winter day. Add a blob of (real) butter, a dollop of brown sauce, find some nice rolls, and you have a satisfying meal. Elisha asks his servant to make some stew or, more likely, a soup. In a time of famine, the idea would have been to gather whatever was possible, mix it together and make something edible.

One of the best parts of a *Church Session* meeting is when someone says, *'Put the kettle on to boil.'* If, as it seems, Elisha has been teaching these sons of the prophets, then his instructions to put on the pot to boil will be the opportunity to take a little break.

Notice that Elisha asks his servant to put on the *'great pot.'* I want to turn our attention to this *'great pot'* being brought out during a famine. No doubt, a large pot may have been required as there were many mouths to be fed. On the other hand, does it not sound ambitious to bring out a large pot during a famine? Elisha wasn't expecting a shortage of food that day. He had faith to believe that a large pot would be needed and, therefore, filled.

Do you believe God can fill a great pot during a spiritual famine? As you look around at a nation in decline, do you believe He can revive and refresh? Do you believe God can pour showers of blessings on a dry and thirsty land? What about as you look at the church, your family and yourself? Can He do the same in those situations? *Can we look at a famine and see a feast?* Can we look at barrenness and see fruitfulness? Faith is the assurance of things that we cannot see in front of us right now (see Hebrews 11:1). Our expectation during barrenness is not because we are *hoping for the best.* It is because we are trusting a superabundant God Who is able to make a way even in the desert (Isaiah 43:19). The knowledge of His ability feeds our expectation of what God can do. Why not bring out the *great pot* and lift it up in anticipation?

DAY 64

Death In The Ulster Fry?

So they poured out for the men to eat. And it came to pass, as they were eating of the pottage, that they cried out, and said, O you man of God, there is death in the pot. And they could not eat thereof.
2nd Kings 4:40

I was queuing in a café with a friend. We received our food and sat at a table to eat. You have probably had the experience of swallowing and feeling that something has *gone down the wrong way,* and you begin to clear your throat. Jackie started to do this, and around the same time, a woman who had been standing beside us in the queue shouted, *'Oh, I've lost my contact lens!'* Jackie *put two and two together* and thought he had swallowed the contact lens. This made him worse, and he started to panic, thinking he was choking. As his face became redder, I began to panic, too. However, a few seconds later, the lady declared she had found the lens, and suddenly, Jackie seemed to be OK. When it was over, we laughed at how the woman's announcement about her lost contact lens had psychologically made Jackie's condition worse. He thought there was death in the *Ulster Fry.*

Someone gathers herbs for Elisha's stew but unwittingly picks up something poisonous. They shout a warning, *'There's death in the pot!'* We will look at some spiritual lessons about this passage over the next few days, but for now, the main message is that God protected His people that day from harm. He did so, using a prophet who knew what to do in the situation. Elisha didn't panic.

1st Chronicles 12:32 tells us of the children of Issachar who understand the times they live in and know what Israel ought to do. Daniel 11:32 speaks of people who know their God and do great exploits. The world is crying out today for people who know God and His Word. It is crying out for those who do not panic despite the chaos all around but have quiet confidence in God and know what to do. Perhaps you will encounter someone today who is panicking over some life issues. Ask God to give you wisdom and speak His truth into that situation with quiet confidence.

DAY 65

An Alarm System

O you man of God, there is death in the pot.
And they could not eat thereof.
2nd Kings 4:40b

I was at an event many years ago where there was outside catering. A friend and I bought some chicken and chips. After a few moments, he warned me not to eat anything. His chicken had pieces of ice throughout as it wasn't properly cooked. We are glad when people warn us of dangers to our safety.

In this passage, a warning is shouted out about the food, *'There is death in the pot.'* It's good that they quickly realised the danger and alerted Elisha. Similarly, it is good that we fellowship together as believers in Jesus. When we are together, perhaps someone recognises something in our lives that could be dangerous and lovingly warns us. A good reason for all ages of the church to meet together is that an older believer may spot something unhealthy in a younger believer's life, which they experienced many years before themselves. Perhaps they can draw that younger person aside and give guidance regarding that situation. It is also vital for us to have good Christian friends whom we trust enough to lovingly tell us when we are on a shaky pathway in life. Often, we have *blind spots* in our lives or our character, which we do not so readily see ourselves, but a good friend will diplomatically and lovingly point out to us for our own good.

These are good reasons for not neglecting to meet with other believers. We worship, pray, learn, fellowship, and, if necessary, warn together. The four significant warning signals we should listen for in our lives are the Holy Spirit, the Word of God, a sanctified conscience and fellow believers who love us.

In 1st Samuel 20, David and Jonathan set up a warning system whereby David would know if Saul was after his life. Jonathan was someone David could trust. Wisdom sets up a warning system rather than closing the door after the horse has bolted.

DAY 66

What Are You Bringing Into The House?

And one went out into the field to gather herbs, and found a wild vine, and gathered thereof wild gourds his lap full, and came and shred them into the pot of pottage: for they knew them not.
2nd Kings 4:39

Those who were brought up in the 1970s and '80s will remember the following perhaps more than others. As kids, you would go outside to play and come into the house later on for a drink of juice. One of your parents would sniff the air and say, *'You have brought something into the house. Let me see the bottom of your shoes.'* And sure enough, there it was. Some dog had left *'a little parcel'* on the ground, and you had unwittingly walked on it and brought it into the house. Thankfully, kids today don't have to contend so much with that issue, as laws require dog owners to pick up their canine's *'little parcels.'*

Just as you unwittingly brought something smelly back into your house, one of these men innocently brought something poisonous back to put in the pot. As they all gathered together to eat, potentially, their fellowship was in great danger.

Fellowship can come in different forms. It can be between us and God, with fellow believers, or within our families. I want to focus on the guy who brought in the poison. We don't want to *'bring anything in'* that will poison the various fellowships in our lives. While we have the Spirit of God to help us, we must also do our part. Job made a *'covenant with his eyes'* regarding what he looked at (Job 31:1). Be vigilant about what you see, hear, think and do. We can pick up baggage in our lives that we do not even realise we are carrying.

That's why we need to be in touch with God's Word as it shines a light into the dark areas of our souls. By allowing God's Word and Spirit to examine, cleanse and refresh us, we can be a source of blessing to those under our influence. Bring back something good into the house.

DAY 67

Fellowship With God

……there is death in the pot
2nd Kings 2:40b

Did you hear about the elderly couple who hadn't argued for over twenty years? They had both turned off their hearing aids and couldn't hear one another's nagging. They lived in a state of constant bliss. (That's just a joke). We hear of couples who have been married for fifty or sixty years. While they may have had *their moments*, they have enjoyed a close relationship overall. That sounds amazing until you consider the fellowship between God the Father and His Son, Jesus. Throughout all eternity past, they lived in a constant, unbroken fellowship. And it will extend into eternity to come. How amazing.

The most crucial fellowship in our lives is that which we have with the Lord. However, unlike God the Father and God the Son (Who have had this unbroken, eternal fellowship), we are far from perfect. Just as one of the sons of the prophets unwittingly brought poison into the pot, we can allow things into our lives that disturb our fellowship with God. What is the gateway through which this poison can enter? We saw yesterday it can be through the gateway of the eyes. However, the heart is the command centre of our eyes and every other part of our being. Proverbs 4:23 tells us that we need to guard our hearts above all else, for everything to do with our lives flows from there. So, what our eyes look at, for example, is determined by the state of our hearts. What is in the heart determines the things we pursue in life, our priorities, our motives and our very thoughts.

The Bible records that David was a man after God's own heart (1st Samuel 13:14). This verse speaks of David's general disposition. His ongoing goal in life was to seek God's heart (even though we know that at times he failed). *Go through with God*. Seek His heart with all your heart. Like David, you will have ups and downs, but He will give you the grace to persevere. Over time, you will see He is transforming your heart to be more like His.

DAY 68

Fellowship With Family

……there is death in the pot
2nd Kings 2:40b

You constantly look at your watch when you are having a bad day at work. You are on a countdown to going home. If you are away somewhere and feeling sick, you just want to get home into a warm bed. While you may have enjoyed your time abroad during a holiday, there comes a time when you look forward to walking through your front door again. You will be glad to be back home. English Judge Sir Edward Coke wrote in 1628 that a man's home is his castle[14] (same goes for a woman!) That sentiment hasn't really changed in almost six hundred years, nor is it likely to change. There's just something about home.

Home, of course, is the common location where family members live and share their lives. Home is much more than the bricks and mortars of a building. The relationship between each family member makes up the dynamic of this place called home. The harmony that should cement the family unit together may be broken when poison is allowed into the pot of fellowship.

Distrust, disagreements, jealousy, bitterness, misunderstanding, impatience and selfishness are just a few poisons that can creep into the family home and make their way into the pot. There is no foolproof method or special formula to stop this from happening. We live in a sinful world, and sin makes its way into family life as much as any other part of our lives.

Recently, as a church, we have been studying the fruit of the Spirit. I spent the first six weeks looking at the fruit of *love.* Why spend so long? It is listed as the first fruit of the Spirit, and then in 1st Corinthians 13:13, Paul affirms that the greatest gift is love. Paul says we are nothing if we have all the gifts but lack love. The foundation for everything we do in the home (and everywhere else) must be based on love. When love stands guard at our door and rules the house, it will be harder for poison to get its damaging foot in. Love is always a winner.

DAY 69

Church Fellowship

……there is death in the pot
2nd Kings 2:40b

There is a beach on Northern Ireland's east coast called Tyrella Beach. At one time, cars were allowed to drive onto the beach. My mum's cousin, Mamie, husband Jack and daughter Jacqueline were there one particular day, and having a lovely time. However, they didn't realise that the tide was coming in from the far end. *Little by little, it slowly but surely made its way in.* There was full-scale panic when they eventually caught on to what was happening. The water was up as far as the door sill. Disaster was averted as they moved the car just in time. Auntie Mamie was so shocked she lost her voice for the rest of the night!

We look today at poison in the pot of church fellowship. What type of poison comes into our churches? Pride, gossip, slander, and disunity are often the causes of the infamous church split. The poison perhaps started small, but as time passed, it was allowed to go unchecked. *Just like the sea tide, the poison slowly but surely made its way through the congregation.* Sometimes, it is stopped before it is too late, and disaster is averted. Unfortunately, at other times, the church family is engulfed and falls apart.

We saw with family fellowship yesterday that while we are imperfect people, love can help to guard against a lot of the poison that can creep into the church. John says, *'Let us love one another: for love is of God' (1st John 4:7)*. Paul speaks about the love of God being poured out into our hearts by the Holy Ghost (Romans 5:5). Just as an artery can get clogged up and the blood cannot flow through properly, our hearts can get blocked up with bitterness, pride and even hatred. We cannot then be channels of blessing. Paul said that when we walk in the Spirit, we cannot simultaneously carry out the desires of the flesh (Galatians 5:16). It stands to reason. If we are filled with God's Spirit, then surely, we cannot be the carriers of poison into the pot of church fellowship. Let <u>His</u> tide come in and submerge us with His love.

DAY 70

The Removal Of Sin And Guilt

But he said, Then bring meal. And he cast it into the pot;
2nd Kings 4:41a

As a child, I was fascinated to discover that if you placed a dirty two-pence coin in a particular well-known fizzy drink, the coin emerged shiny and spotlessly clean after a few moments. Of course, my parents posed the awkward question: if the fizzy drink did that to the coin, what would it do to our *'insides'?* As we will see in a moment, Jesus can wipe the dirt from our lives and make us completely clean.

The sons of the prophets have called on Elisha for help. He asks them to bring some meal (or flour) and throws it into the pot. We then read that there is no more harm in the pot. What a strange thing to do. How did throwing flour into the pot take away the poison? As we saw with Elijah's mantle, there was nothing special about the mantle. It was only symbolic. The actual power was from God Himself, which flowed through the prophet. It is just the same with anointing oil. James 5:14 instructs us to call the church elders if we are sick and to allow them to anoint us with oil. There is no power in the oil. James says to anoint, *'In the Name of the Lord.'* This is the source of the power and not the oil itself.

There is symbolism in this story. One of Israel's sacrificial offerings was called the meal offering. The meal (or flour) in that offering can be seen as a picture of Jesus, Who is the *Bread of Life.* When the Bread of Life is allowed to deal with the poison (sin) that comes into our lives, He takes the poison away. 1st John 1:7 reminds us, *'The Blood of Jesus Christ His Son cleanses us from all sin.'* If you have eaten contaminated food, you may remember how you suffered after-effects for some days. Jesus not only cleanses us but also takes away the after-effects. He takes away the guilt. As Isaiah stood one day in that Holy place, he was given the assurance that not only had his sin been dealt with, but his iniquity *(guilt)* had also been taken away (Isaiah 6:7). Take time to thank God that your sin and your guilt have been completely removed.

DAY 71

Taking God At His Word

.....and he said, Pour out for the people, that they may eat.
2nd Kings 4:41b

What about this recipe? Chop some sausages and pineapple into a saucepan of baked beans (make sure not to let the beans dry up). Then add cashew nuts. Serve on a plate of boiled rice. My family refuse to eat it. They call it *'muck'* for some reason. That was the general reaction of others from our church, although I must report that one couple tried it and said it *'wasn't bad.'* I count that as a victory.

It may take a lot of faith to eat my '*muck,'* but would you have had the confidence to eat from Elisha's pot after he declared it was safe to eat? Imagine you were there and watched him throwing flour into the poisonous pot. It isn't recorded that anything visible took place, yet Elisha says it's ready to eat. Who would have been the first person to try it? Someone with a lot of faith! Someone who would believe what Elisha had said.

In Matthew 8, a centurion came to Jesus asking that his servant would be healed. Jesus replied that He would come and heal him. The centurion countered that all Jesus had to do was to speak the Word, and his servant would be healed. The man was willing to believe for healing, even though he would not see it until returning home. He was willing to take Jesus at His Word. As Thomas proclaimed in wonder, *'My Lord and my God,'* he had seen Jesus and believed. However, Jesus pronounces a blessing upon those who have not seen and yet have believed (John 20:28-29).

As a child of God, there is a blessing upon your life because you have stepped out into salvation and taken God at His Word. Those who continue to *go through with God* will constantly be called upon to believe things they cannot see. We sometimes call it *the eye of faith.* It is also called *taking God at His Word.* When you board an aircraft, you cannot physically see the engine, but you believe it has the power to bring you to your destination. How much more can you trust Jesus to bring you through?

DAY 72

The Transforming Power Of God

And there was no harm in the pot.
2nd Kings 4:41c

Di and I were married in 2007, and six weeks later, I ended up in hospital. (The two incidents are not related)! I joked afterwards that I was testing Di's wedding vows, which mentioned, *'In sickness and in health.'* I wasn't joking in the hospital, though. The pain was intense, and something needed to be done. I soon discovered that I had a severely inflamed appendix, which had to be removed. The transformation (from extreme pain to eventually no pain at all after full recovery) was striking. The pain from the appendix had no more power over me once it was removed.

The transformation in this story is also striking. One moment, there is food in a pot that is unsafe to touch. Death could even occur. But once the pot came into contact with the power of God, it became completely safe. The power of God removed the danger of the poison, and now we read there was *'No harm in the pot.'* It had no more power of fear over the sons of the prophets

That's what God's power does. It takes a life full of the poison of sin and, because of what Jesus did on the cross, makes the sinner completely righteous (positionally) in the eyes of God. What a transformation. The power of sin is broken. When a Christian comes to die, and the mourners are gathered around a coffin, they are reminded that these are just the remains of a body, and their loved one is, at that very moment, enjoying the presence of Jesus. You see, the power of God removes the poison and the sting of death so that we can declare, *'O death, where is your sting, O grave, where is your victory?'* (1st Corinthians 15:55). The power of death is broken.

God's power can transform someone who is full of worry, anxiety, fear, guilt and bitterness by removing these things and filling them with God's peace and power, taking away the harm. Ask for His power to transform you today.

SECTION 7

THERE CAME A MAN

2nd Kings 4:42-44

DAY 73

God Will Provide

And there came a man from Baalshalisha, and brought the man of God bread of the firstfruits, twenty loaves of barley, and full ears of corn in the husk thereof.
2nd Kings 4:42a

Dad had open heart surgery when he was just a young man of around thirty-one years old. He subsequently suffered from some strokes, which left him paralysed down his left side. In those early years especially, he was constantly very ill. It was a blow for Dad when he could no longer bring in a wage due to his condition. Mum became a stay-at-home carer, and they had to bring up two young children while depending on government benefits (which, compared to today, were not as substantial). However, their dependence was not solely on the government but primarily on the Lord. In times of difficulty, I can still hear Mum's words ringing in my ears: *'The Lord hasn't let us down up until now, and He isn't going to.'* On numerous occasions, an envelope would come through the door containing cash or a cheque. Sometimes, we knew who the giver was; other times, they were anonymous. God always provided for us, no matter what the circumstances were like.

We have learned already from this chapter that the nation is experiencing famine. This passage will recount a story similar to the New Testament miracles where Jesus fed five thousand on one occasion and four thousand on another. Although this particular account involves a smaller sample of people (one hundred men), it is still an incredible testimony of God's provision for His people. You will notice that most of the miracles we have looked at so far are in connection with God supplying the simple needs of people. We wonder why an Almighty God Who rules this universe would be so interested in the seemingly small and basic things that are so important to us. Jesus reminds us that since He cares for the sparrows and the lilies in the fields, how much more does He care for us? (Matthew 6:26-30). God will provide.

DAY 74

Never Had It So Good

And there came a man from Baalshalisha, and brought the man of God bread of the firstfruits, twenty loaves of barley, and full ears of corn in the husk thereof.
2nd Kings 4:42a

In 1957, UK Prime Minister Harold Macmillan's government declared, '*You never had it so good.*'[15] Some twelve years had passed since the *Second World War*, and the nation was beginning to bounce back again. As we continue to think about God's provision for His people (which is really the theme of this passage), we are inclined to think of God's supply in terms of material things, but what about His spiritual provision?

One of the most striking stories from the Old Testament is that of Abraham and Isaac in Genesis 22. As they made their way up that mountain, it must have been a challenging walk for Abraham. Isaac innocently points out that there is wood and fire, but where is the lamb for the burnt offering? Probably not even knowing that he was speaking prophetically, Abraham answered that God would provide a lamb. What a moment it must have been as Isaac watched the provided sacrifice dying on that altar in his place. What a picture of the Lamb of God, Jesus, taking our place on Calvary's cross. Abraham called that momentous place '*Jehovah-Jireh*' (which means *the Lord will provide*).

We can truly say that since the moment we got saved (spiritually speaking), we have *never had it so good.* We have been blessed with all spiritual blessings in Jesus Christ (Ephesians 1:3), seated in Heavenly places with Him (Ephesians 2:6), justified in His Name (1st Corinthians 6:11), been made a new creation (2nd Corinthians 5:17), made alive to God (Romans 6:11) and made heirs with God and joint-heirs with Christ (Romans 8:17). I have only scratched the surface here. All of these things, and more, were provided by the death of Jesus Christ. When you are tempted to be discouraged by a lack of material things, remember the richness of God's provision for you in Jesus.

DAY 75

Sent From God

And there came a man from Baalshalisha....
2nd Kings 4:42a

Not everyone knows that Portrush was bombed during the period known as *the Troubles*. I was there, so I remember it well. It was August 1976, and we stayed there as a family in a Bed and Breakfast accommodation. On the day of the bombing, two ladies my Grandmother knew turned up to see us unexpectedly, and we went with them to Portstewart. While we were there that evening, the bombs began to go off in Portrush. As we came back to Portrush, the place was in chaos. Police were trying to get people to go to the beach for safety. We could see the fire burning and the smoke rising. However, we believe God sent those two ladies to take us away that day, so we weren't in the centre of it all when the evacuation and the chaos began. We ended up sleeping that night in the local school. It is something I will never forget.

We read earlier in verse 38 that there was a famine in the land. We also know that the nation was far from God. In the middle of the darkness of famine and idolatry, we read, *'There came a man.'* He comes with food for Elisha. No doubt, you can recall (maybe it was your darkest night and in your deepest need) when God sent someone your way. Maybe they came with a word of comfort or encouragement, which you needed at that moment. Maybe someone posted cash through your letterbox in a time of financial need. Perhaps someone stalled you from going somewhere, and you avoided a catastrophe. We know some should have been at the *World Trade Centre* during the terror attacks of 2001, but due to a last-minute change of plan, they were called away.

As you recall people who were planted in a particular place, and you know beyond the shadow of a doubt that they were sent by God, why not take time to thank the Lord for His goodness? It was His care, love, mercy and grace that sent them. Remembering His past goodness builds up your faith for days ahead.

DAY 76

Hearing His Voice

And there came a man from Baalshalisha.....
2nd Kings 4:42a

I knew that the Lord had been speaking very loudly to my heart earlier that morning. I was in secular employment at the time and (having finished early due to a work incentive) stopped in a café. A lady clearing the tables dropped a tray, and everything crashed around her. The sound of broken dishes seemed to magnify in my mind, and I knew in my spirit that this was what God had been speaking to me about earlier: brokenness. I felt the Lord was telling me to go to the lady and speak a word to her about brokenness. I didn't want to. I would look stupid. She would think I am crazy. I resisted, but the prompting to speak to her would not shift. I *put out a fleece* and said that if she came back onto the café floor before I left, I would speak to her (I was sort of hoping she wouldn't!) But she came out. I sheepishly told her what I felt the Lord had put on my heart. She didn't laugh or mock. I could see in her eyes that it meant something. Six (or more) years later, I don't know what the purpose was, but I leave it with God.

Yesterday, we recalled how others have been sent to help us in the past. But what if God is calling *you* to be *that man* or *that woman* to help someone else in need? You will have to be open to God's voice. Jesus said, *'My sheep hear My voice'* (John 10:27). You will also need a heart of obedience. Sometimes, there will be a struggle from within as you grapple with your assignment. Ananias struggled as the Lord told him to go and meet with Saul of Tarsus (as his name struck fear into the hearts of believers at that time). He eventually relented and went. You must also be prepared to surrender your rationale to the Lord. Ananias indicated how unusual the idea sounded and told the Lord about how much evil Saul had done. Did God not know already? Of course, He did! Who is God calling you to help or speak to today? As long as you are sure it is the Lord speaking to you, then no matter how crazy it sounds, simply obey.

DAY 77

What's In A Name?

And there came a man from Baalshalisha.....
2nd Kings 4:42a

What's in a name? A while back, the name of a country lane caught my attention and gave me a bit of a laugh. It was called *'Hungry House Lane.'* It reminds me of our house when the kids return from school and raid the cupboards and fridge. In those mad moments, our home becomes a *hungry house*! It's not as if they aren't fed at school, by the way! They are just so full of energy.

We don't place much meaning on names today. But back in Bible times, names were very significant. Often, they would reflect someone's character or be linked with an incident that had occurred. One meaning for Jacob's name was *'deceiver,'* and it reflected his character. God, however, changed his name to Israel, which can mean *'Prince with God'* (Genesis 32:28). When Rachel, after many years, gave birth, she called the boy Joseph (meaning, *'The Lord adds'*). In doing so, she called on the Lord to add another son (who would eventually be Benjamin).

'There came a man from Baalshalisha.' This place is mentioned in 1st Samuel 9:4 regarding a better time in Saul's life, just before he was anointed as the first king of Israel. However, in Saul's day, it was called *Shalisha*. Here, the name *'Baal'* has been added (the name of a false god). The name Baalshalisha indicates that this area has been given over to idolatry. The encouraging thing to note is that, from a place associated with idolatry and darkness, there comes a man who is active for God (despite the apostasy all around). He didn't just sit back and think, *'Well, everything around me is getting worse; there's no point in trying to do anything for God.'* No. This man is in touch with God and ready to shine his light in a darkened world. We live in strangely dark times. Don't be influenced by the environment around you; but by the mighty God within you. Listen for His voice, *go through with God*, shine your light and do great exploits for Him.

DAY 78

Good Stewards

And there came a man from Baalshalisha, and brought the man of God bread of the firstfruits, twenty loaves of barley, and full ears of corn in the husk thereof.
2nd Kings 4:42

Our girls think they own the TV. Ellie, especially, will usually take the remote control and hide it under the cushion (or under the sofa or inside a drawer) so that she is in complete command and can watch her cartoons. The irritating thing is when the girls have hidden the remote control, and they can't remember where they put it. When they speak about *their* TV and *their* remote control, I remind them who paid for it all!

Just as I have to remind my kids who owns what, the Bible gently reminds us in verses like Psalm 24:1 that the Earth and everything within it belongs to the Lord. We read that this man who came from Baalshalisha brings to Elisha the '*Bread of the first fruits.*' What is that? When God's people would come into the land they had inherited, and the first harvest was produced, before they did anything, they had to give back to God a portion of that new produce (see Leviticus 23:9-14). They were acknowledging that the land they harvested primarily belonged to God. So, this was a thank-offering to God, reminding them that He was their provider. The day we lose our gratitude to God is when we go on a downhill slide spiritually. Cultivate a thankful heart.

This man from Baalshalisha kept aside the first fruits of his produce (acknowledging God as his provider) and brought them as a gift to Elisha. He was a good steward of what God had given to him. He didn't bring it to the apostate priests who had departed from God and dabbled in idolatry. He honoured God by bringing it to Elisha. The Lord also wants us to be good stewards of what He has given us. That includes being good stewards not only of our finances but of our time and talents. When we acknowledge that God has given us these things in the first place, we will find it easier to give them back to Him with a grateful heart.

DAY 79

Giving Back To God

And there came a man from Baalshalisha, and brought the man of God bread of the firstfruits, twenty loaves of barley, and full ears of corn in the husk thereof.
2nd Kings 4:42

To tithe or not to tithe? That is the question on the lips of many in the church world. As we continue to look at being good stewards of what God has given us, it is perhaps needful to look at this (at times) controversial subject. Yesterday, I laid the foundation: everything on the Earth is the Lord's. The first fruits established a principle that we should give a portion back to God by way of thanksgiving. That Old Testament principle is carried over into the New Testament. In 1st Corinthians 16:2, Paul instructs believers: *'Upon the first day of the week let every one of you lay by him in store, as God has prospered him, that there be no gatherings when I come.'* I think the crucial phrase there is, '*As God has prospered him.'*

In the Old Testament, the tithe was generally reckoned to be a tenth. When tithing is mentioned in the church, two objections at least are given. Firstly, we are a people under grace, and tithing brings us back into the law. Secondly, the tithe mentioned in Malachi 3:10 speaks of food, not money. While this is true, we mustn't miss the principle here. Tithing was in operation before the law (Abraham and Jacob both tithed). Although food was mainly involved in the tithe, *the principal is giving back to God.* The tenth, I believe, should only be used as a guideline and not as a law. If you aren't sure how much to give, then give a tenth. It's a good place to start. The danger of this, however, is that we can get into a mindset of paying a tenth and then determining the rest is mine! '*I've given my part.'* But, as mentioned earlier, we are people of grace, and grace means you can give more! Paul reminds us that God loves a cheerful giver, and we should not give grudgingly or because we feel we have to (2nd Corinthians 9:7). The main point is that God has blessed us, and we should willingly give back to Him with thankful hearts. God is no man's debtor.

DAY 80

The Testing Of Our Faith

And he said, Give to the people, that they may eat.
2nd Kings 2:42b

Nobody likes tests, but they are essential in all walks of life so we can discover how much we understand a particular subject. Sometimes, the waiting period before the test is more nerve-racking than the test itself. That was the case for me as I awaited my driving test. I was a bundle of nerves. When the actual test came (along with some other tasks), I was asked to complete a *three-point turn* on a road that was wide enough to do a *U-turn.* It couldn't have worked out better. Also, those were the days when you didn`t do a written theory test. I was asked three questions from the *Highway Code*, and that was it. Wouldn't it be great if all our tests were as simple as that?

If you are to *go through with God*, you can expect to be tested. As we have seen already, digging ditches (when there is no prospect of water) will test our faith. In today's verse, Elisha asks his servant to feed one hundred mouths when it is clear that there is not enough food.

Testing our faith is essential. When we are tested, God is not watching us in expectation that we will fall flat on our faces. The Bible describes our faith as *'More precious than gold that perishes'* (1st Peter 1:7). Gold will not last forever but needs to be tested in the fire. When our faith is tested, it is with the view that it will last throughout eternity. James 1:3 says that testing our faith produces patience (or endurance). Tests come not to destroy our faith but that it may grow and keep on going.

Was Elisha testing his servant to see if he would say, *'We haven't enough food, but God can provide'?* We will see tomorrow that his first instinct was to look at the lack of food. Perhaps you will be tested today. Your first instinct may be to think something is impossible because of *what there is not.* But God's Word says that things become impossible only when *faith* is lacking (Hebrews 11:6). Faith always trumps whatever you may lack.

DAY 81

Focus On What You Have

And his servitor said,
What, should I set this before a hundred men?
2nd Kings 4:43a

Especially in the early days of Dad's illness, people were always calling in and out of the house to visit. Mum loved to have people around and thrived on hospitality. That was her *'thing.'* Mothers especially have this uncanny ability to make food stretch. When people would call in unexpectedly, Mum could make a meal originally intended for five people stretch out to feed an extra two or three. It was like a miracle!

The man from Baalshalisha has brought food for Elisha. However, others are present (the sons of the prophets), and the obvious concern of Elisha's servant is that there isn't enough to feed one hundred mouths. He is astounded that Elisha should ask him to feed them with this small supply.

We saw something similar in the story of the widow and the oil. We need to come to God with the little that we have and give it to Him. We must also learn this lesson in the spiritual realm as we look at ourselves and feel that we have very little to give to God. It is a human trait to focus on what we *lack* rather than what we *already have.* A constant focus on what we *do not have* will only lead to discouragement and even self-loathing. As we look around at others and see their giftings and talents being used, it can make matters worse.

What we should do (rather than focus on what we *lack*) is to bring the little that we *have* to the Lord (along with our faith). As you ponder over what you think you *lack* (which is holding you back from serving God), why not take a piece of paper and write down what you *do have?* If you really think long and hard about it, I suspect you may be surprised that you have gifts and talents that you didn't realise before. Pray over that list. Dedicate it to God and ask Him to use those things that you *do have* for His glory.

DAY 82

What Makes You Sit Up And Listen?

.....he said again, Give the people, that they may eat:
for thus says the LORD, They shall eat, and shall leave thereof.
2nd Kings 2:43b

'G*irls, tidy your room.' 'Girls, eat your food.' 'Girls, do your homework.'* Silence reigns. Nothing happens. *'Not a creature was stirring, not even a mouse.'*[16]

'OK, girls. One, two, three, four....' and before I reach five, they are doing what I have asked. What made the difference? When I start counting to five, they know there will be consequences, so they sit up and listen. Of course, they must learn to do what they are told without counting to five! But that is a work in progress.

What makes you sit up and listen? For Elisha's servant, it was the Word of the Lord. You see, Elisha told him the first time to give the men food to eat. No doubt, Elisha's servant greatly respected his master, but this instruction seemed impossible. As good as your mother may have been at stretching the food (see *Day 81*), this was too big of a stretch! There was no way that one hundred men could be fed in this way. The servant doesn`t even have the faith to believe Elisha, the great prophet of God. Elisha repeats a second time to give them to eat, and then he adds, *'Thus says the Lord.'* God had instructed that they would all eat and food would be left over. That Word of authority from God changed the whole situation entirely. Now he obeys.

Does God's Word make us sit up and listen? Does the final authority of His Word change our thinking? One moment, you may be listening to your own thoughts, fearful of what lies ahead and doubting in your heart, but suddenly, His Word changes the situation. God's Word can lift you from defeat to victory, discouragement to encouragement and uncertainty to assurance. Those who will *go through with God* rely on His voice. They listen for His voice. They thirst to hear His voice. His Word is like fire in their bones (Jeremiah 20:9). They say, *'Speak Lord for Your servant is listening'* (see 1st Samuel 3:10).

DAY 83

Bring God Into The Equation

.....he said again, Give the people, that they may eat:
for thus says the LORD, They shall eat, and shall leave thereof.
2nd Kings 2:43

If you are reading this first thing in the morning, you will love what I am going to do next. Here is a lovely equation for you to mull over with your coffee. If $x + y = z$ (with x being *five* and z being *twelve),* everything else will be wrong if you leave *seven* out of the equation. When the servant left God out of the equation, he couldn`t get things to work out. There was no way on this Earth that he could make x + y = z with the little food that he had. As we saw yesterday, it all changed with the authority of God's Word as the Lord was brought into the equation.

As we puzzle over the complexities of life, there is no way we can make things add up unless we bring God into the equation. (Let me add: there are things in life that we will never understand this side of Heaven. It seems some things will never add up. But bringing God into the equation and trusting His Word gives us peace and comfort despite the problems we are facing).

You may be discouraged today as you feel that your life seems to be yourself against the world. Bring God into the equation, and you will find strength in the fact that 'If God be for us, who can be against us?' (Romans 8:31). You may feel as if you are almost drowning beneath the storms of life. It may seem like the flames of the trials of this life are surrounding you. Bring God into the equation, and be comforted because He says that the waters shall not overflow you, the fire shall not burn you, and He will be with you (Isaiah 43:2). Maybe you feel like your life is crumbling beneath and all around you. Bring God into the equation, and you will take heart that underneath you are His everlasting arms (Deuteronomy 33:27). It is so easy to be weighed down by the different problems in our lives and to try to find a solution for ourselves. We can switch to panic mode and feel out of control. Whatever you are facing today, *bring God into the equation.*

DAY 84

Seek Jesus Above Everything Else

So he set it before them, and they did eat, and left thereof, according to the word of the LORD.
2nd Kings 4:44

Dad could only whisper for around thirteen years due to one of the strokes which he suffered. It seems that the stroke damaged the part of the brain that sends messages to the voice box, causing a rare form of *vocal cord paralysis*. In the early years, due to the severity of his illness, he spent a lot of time upstairs. An intercom system was placed in his bedroom and the kitchen. If Mum was needed, he would buzz the intercom, and she would answer that she was on her way. One particular morning, Dad was reading a Psalm, and his voice miraculously returned. He immediately buzzed the intercom, and Mum replied she was coming. Using his newly restored voice, Dad then said, *'Lorna, I love you.'* Mum probably broke the world record for running up the stairs! What a blessing that Dad could speak again.

This passage recounting a miracle of multiplied food (with lots left over) reminds me of the feeding of five thousand people. After the event, Jesus perceived that they wanted to make Him king. They were following Jesus because of what they could get out of Him. So, He went to a mountain to be alone.

I strongly believe that God still works miracles today. But let's seek Jesus primarily for Who He is rather than for what we can *get out of Him.* God miraculously moved as Dad got his speech back. Other amazing things also happened in his life that were undoubtedly interventions from God. Yet Dad was disabled for around forty years, spending most of that time in a wheelchair. He never received the miracle to be able to walk again, even though he was prayed for all across this country and even abroad. But for Dad, his relationship with Jesus was more important than even getting his miracle. It was secondary; Jesus was first. Dad displayed that principle throughout his life. Miracles and answers to prayer are great, but seek Jesus above all else.

SECTION 8

LINKS IN THE CHAIN

2nd Kings 5:1-27

DAY 85

There's Always A 'But'

Now Naaman, captain of the host of the king of Syria,
was a great man with his master, and honourable,
because by him the LORD had given deliverance to Syria:
he was also a mighty man in valour, but he was a leper.
2nd Kings 5:1

You are attending a training session, and the time comes to assess what you have learned. The leader praises your understanding, telling you how well you have done. You are beginning to feel like *the best thing since sliced loaf* when the word *'but'* crosses the leader's lips. You should have known better because, as the saying goes, *there's always a 'but.'*

Naaman is the leading star in the opening of chapter 5. Verse 1 sings his praises. If he had been alive in the last century, he would have had the status of someone like the famous Generals Eisenhower or MacArthur. God had used Naaman to bring deliverance to Syria. You see, God can even use pagans like Pharaoh, Nebuchadnezzar and Cyrus for His glory. Naaman is well-liked, courageous and even described as honourable. Just when it seems like the accolades cannot get any higher, we are confronted with that three-letter word. Yes, there is always a *'but.'* We discover life is not as rosy as it seems for Naaman. He is a leper. This *'but'* reminds us that everyone is vulnerable no matter how good we think we are or how well life seems to be going. There is a *'but'* in everyone's life. Your problem will differ from someone else's problem, but we all have needs for which the Lord is the only answer.

The story of Naaman is a fascinating one about how this great soldier deals with the *'but'* in his life. Although he almost didn't '*make it'* (at times, he was his own worst enemy), Naaman's story encourages those seeking to *go through with God*. Sometimes, we can also be our own worst enemy, but despite our failures along the way, God is patient with us. Don't give up.

DAY 86

A Link In The Chain

And the Syrians had gone out by companies,
and had brought away captive out of the land of Israel a little maid;
and she waited on Naaman's wife.
2nd Kings 5:2

Di and I bought bikes around fourteen years ago. We began enthusiastically at first, but within a year, they were no longer being used. They sit today in the shed gathering dust. The chain on mine has completely rusted. I have grand ideas of sorting the chain out, but one summer turns into another, and nothing happens. It's funny, but cyclists will talk about the overall shape of their bike, the seat, the brakes, the gears, the pedals or the wheels, but rarely about the chain. There are over one hundred tiny links in the average bicycle chain.[17] They seem so insignificant, yet the bike is going nowhere without the chain.

Links in the chain are so important in the story of Naaman. As he plods along, trying to find his way to a cure, he is helped by vital links in the chain. Each link brings him nearer and nearer to his answer. We have already observed that the link in a chain seems so tiny and negligible. The first link in Naaman's chain is so insignificant that hardly anyone would notice her. She is a Hebrew slave. Yet she is that vital first link which starts him on his journey to *go through with God.*

The contrast between the mighty Naaman and this insignificant little Hebrew slave girl could not be more striking. This girl is a living and breathing example of 1st Corinthians 1:27. *'But God has chosen the foolish things of the world to confound the wise; and God has chosen the weak things of the world to confound the things which are mighty.'* Who would ever take this little girl under their notice? Yet she is going to influence the future of one of the greatest men in the land. To everyone else, you may be an insignificant *nobody*, but to Heaven, as a child of God, you are a *somebody*. Ask God how you can be a link in the chain of someone's life today.

DAY 87

Cling To Jesus

And she said to her mistress, Would God my lord were with the prophet that is in Samaria! for he would recover him of his leprosy.
2nd Kings 5:3

Granny McKinley's husband and father died within six weeks of each other. She was left as a single parent to bring up a twelve-year-old girl. When Granny was in her fifties, she had a heart attack. Her response was to learn to drive a car! Then, in her sixties, Granny was diagnosed with breast cancer. Despite all that, she lived for another thirty years to the grand old age of ninety-three. Life had been tough, but she kept her faith in God and, with His help, battled her way through the adversities which she faced.

This little Hebrew girl had great adversity in her life. Having been taken captive from the land of Israel, she was now a slave in Syria. She most likely had been separated from her family. Think of the heartache she must be going through. Think of the questions she will be grappling with in her mind. Her story reminds us that we are not exempt from life's troubles when we *go through with God.* In fact, you may find that when you are determined to follow relentlessly after God, adversity seems to increase at times.

It is thought that Psalm 63 was written when David's son Absalom was trying to usurp his own father's throne. In the middle of all this, David declares, *'My soul follows hard after you'* (verse 8). What he is really saying is that his soul clings to God. In times when adversity increases, cling to God, don't run from Him.

Despite what this girl had suffered, she was not bitter towards God. Imagine if she had allowed bitterness to consume her heart. Would she have cared whether her captor (Naaman) lived or died? Would she have told him that there was a prophet of God who could heal him? I don't think so. Bitterness towards God tends to suck His fire out of the soul. But here is a young girl who still retains her passion for God. You can, too. When adversity comes, cling all the more to Jesus. He can keep that fire burning.

DAY 88

One Sentence That Changed Naaman's Destiny

And one went in, and told his lord, saying,
Thus and thus said the maid that is of the land of Israel.
2nd Kings 5:4

Our kids' school presents Christmas shows for the parents, performed over a few days by different classes. They usually do a nativity play along with some songs. While the parents enjoy the show, the main focus is their child. They may only have one line to say or perhaps even one word. It could just be a sheep's bleat or a cow's moo. Each parent waits with bated breath for their little star to perform. That one line they speak is (for them) worthy of an *Oscar*. As the child walks away from the microphone, their loved ones wipe away the tears and proudly clap as if there is no tomorrow.

This little Hebrew girl has only *one line to speak in the entire Bible,* and how well she does it. Then she disappears out of view. Undoubtedly, her Heavenly Father looked down on her that day with great pleasure as this little slave witnessed about the power of God, which was present in Israel through Elisha. This one sentence was the spark which set Naaman off on a journey that would see him eventually *go through with God.*

Please get this. Based on what this Hebrew slave said, Naaman goes to the highest power in the land (the king of Syria) with a report of her words, hoping that something can be done. Why would Naaman (one of the most influential men in Syria) listen to someone who is regarded as the lowest of the low? She is only an insignificant Hebrew slave. Why would he take any heed at all of what she would say? I believe it was because there was something about her. I put it to you that while Naaman observed how she conducted herself as a captive in enemy territory, he saw something of her God in her life. It is surely the only valid explanation. If those who observe our lives daily see something of the Lord in us, then the words we speak may just be the spark that sets them on a journey to *go through with God.*

DAY 89

Bring Them To Me

And it was so, when Elisha the man of God had heard that the king of Israel had rent his clothes, that he sent to the king, saying, Why have you rent your clothes? let him come now to me, and he shall know that there is a prophet in Israel.
2nd Kings 5:8

A man was stopped one day by the police. The officer said, *'Do you know that you are driving up a one-way street?'* The man replied, *'Sure, I'm only going the one way anyway!'* The officer wasn't too impressed by the answer.

There is only one way, and it is God's way. Any other way is the wrong direction. Having started well by heeding the words of the Hebrew slave, unfortunately, Naaman takes a turn in the wrong direction. Let's remember, though, that Naaman is a new seeker of God and is finding his way. He goes to the king of Israel with money as he pursues healing but has come to the wrong place. The king can't help him, thinks he is looking for a quarrel and tears his clothes angrily. Naaman is a picture of the person seeking life's answers in the wrong places. He could find no cure for his sickness in the king's palace, just as humanity can find no cure for brokenness and sin outside of Jesus. But just as it seems that Naaman has lost his way, Elisha becomes a second link in the chain. He hears what has happened and says, *'Let him come now to me, and he shall know that there is a prophet in Israel.'*

Elisha here displays two qualities of a person who *goes through with God.* Firstly, he is eager to draw this God-seeker close to him so he can influence him for good. He wants to take Naaman away from the wrong path and point him in the right direction. Who is it you can walk alongside today and influence for God? Secondly, Elisha wants him to know there is a prophet in Israel (not for his own fame, but he wants Naaman to experience the power of God). Do you long that others may know God's salvation, power and glory in their lives? As you see the lost walking in the wrong direction today, will you say, like Elisha, *'Bring them to me'*?

DAY 90

I Thought

But Naaman was angry, and went away, and said, Behold, I thought, he will surely come out to me, and stand, and call on the name of the Lord his God, and strike his hand over the place, and recover the leper.
2nd Kings 5:11

As kids, we often incorrectly assumed or presumed certain things. On such occasions, Dad would normally quip, *'You know what 'thought' did. It planted a feather and thought a hen would grow.'* We used to laugh at that, but wrong thinking can have serious consequences. Two cars collide because one driver thought he had plenty of time to pull out of a junction. He didn't. Two friends fall out because one thought the other's comment was *a joke with a jag.* It wasn't. The guys thought their seemingly carefree mate could pull himself back up after a series of circumstances went against him. He couldn't.

You can imagine the dramatic scene. Naaman screeches to a halt with his horses and chariot outside Elisha's door. The prophet doesn't even greet this influential soldier but sends his servant to tell him to dip in the River Jordan seven times, and he would be healed. You can almost see Naaman's body shake with rage. In verse 11, he says, *'I thought.'* What did he think? He expected Elisha to dramatically call on God, strike out his hand and heal Naaman. He wanted the pomp and ceremony that befitted his rank.

One of the great dangers in the Christian life is when we try to *second-guess* God. We think he should do things a certain way. When we pray about something, often without even realising, we tell God how He should do it. As humans, we like to be in control and attempt to exert our influence over the One Who takes counsel from no one. He gently reminds us in Isaiah 55:8 that His thoughts are not our thoughts. Those who wish to *go through with God* can better understand the Almighty's thoughts by immersing their hearts and minds in His Word. Next time we presume to think we know what God is doing or how He should do it, let's stop and pray, *'Show me Your ways, O LORD'* (Psalm 25:4).

DAY 91

The Danger Of Pride

Are not Abana and Pharpar, rivers of Damascus, better than all the waters of Israel? may I not wash in them, and be clean? So he turned and went away in a rage.
2nd Kings 2:12

The kids and I were coming from the local swimming pool. I have trainers with exceptionally long laces (I don`t know why they make them that way). The laces had come loose, and I stepped on one. I didn`t just trip but was catapulted forward. My phone flew out of my hand in what seemed like slow motion, my glasses case slid across the floor, and down I went. People ran over to check if I was OK. It was kind of them, but I just wanted to get away without a fuss. Whatever way I had fallen, my hands hurt for weeks after. But the worst part is when your pride is hurt.

Naaman left Elisha's house in a rage for two reasons. His thinking was wrong (which we saw yesterday), and his heart was full of pride. Elisha's servant had told Naaman to wash in the Jordan seven times. He was incensed by this instruction. Surely the rivers of Damascus in Syria were far superior to this dirty River Jordan in Israel? His pride had also been hurt because Elisha stayed in his house and didn't make a big fuss over this Syrian celebrity.

Proverbs 6:16-19 tells us that seven things are an abomination to God. Pride heads that list and is the root cause of most wars, marriage problems, family breakdowns, church disagreements and community friction. Naaman almost misses his blessing due to his pride over the location of a river. He turns away in a rage. James 4:6 informs us that God resists the proud. Naaman, who had begun well in seeking God, was now at risk of putting himself in direct opposition to God. For the person who will *go through with God*, pride must be crucified on a daily basis. We can, however, be encouraged that while God resists the proud, the other half of the verse says He gives grace to the humble. Don't miss out on what God has for you due to pride. Take the posture of humility and watch His grace pour out over your life.

DAY 92

The Voice Of Reason

And his servants came near, and spoke to him, and said, My father, if the prophet had bid you do some great thing, would you not have done it? how much rather then, when he says to you, Wash, and be clean?
2nd Kings 5:13

I was a bit apprehensive about attending Bible College when I was in my 40s, especially since the last time I had studied academically was for my A-levels many years before. There were many times I had to *burn the midnight oil* and moments when I felt like giving it up. Di would have been my *voice of reason,* encouraging me to keep going on. There are times when, in moments of panic, discouragement or even anger, we determine to go down a route that isn't really for the best. Someone speaks reason into the situation, and we pull back. Imagine how different our lives might have been had that person not spoken into our circumstances. We should thank God for those words of wisdom.

Naaman is about to throw away this golden opportunity for his life to be dramatically changed, all because of his pride. Thankfully, his servants become a third link in the chain (the Hebrew girl and Elisha being the previous two) and become the *voice of reason* in his life. Their rationale is that if Elisha had asked Naaman to do something challenging to receive his healing, he would have done it. Why, then, could he not do this simple thing?

The apostle Paul was a *voice of reason.* In Acts 17:2, Paul came to a synagogue in Thessalonica, and on three occasions, he *reasoned with them* from the Scriptures. People around us today are scared and confused and don't know what to do. Be the *voice of reason.* Use those things you have learned over the years through the Scriptures to speak into their lives for good. In Acts 24:25, Paul *reasoned* with Felix about righteousness, self-control and the judgment to come. Felix trembled that day but, unfortunately, procrastinated. At least Paul tried. Someone out there today in your sphere of influence needs a guiding hand. Come alongside them and be that loving *voice of reason.*

DAY 93

Obedience Matters

Then went he down, and dipped himself seven times in Jordan, according to the saying of the man of God: and his flesh came again like to the flesh of a little child, and he was clean.
2nd Kings 5:14

One number can make all the difference. When Ellie was a toddler, the doorbell rang one evening. It was the police. They received a *999* call from our house (in the UK, that is the emergency services' phone number). When we explained the situation, everything was OK. Ellie, of course, did not even know what *999* meant. What were the chances she would dial three nines in a row? Even if she had dialled *998*, just one number short, all would have been fine. But she dialled two nines, and that final digit was the trigger to send out the police.

As I mentioned yesterday, Naaman had been influenced by three links in the chain. He had also overcome the obstacles of an angry king, his own perceptions of how God would heal him, and his pride. (By the way, pride is usually one of the last obstacles broken down before God's blessings have the freedom to flow). But there is one more thing needed to complete the miracle. Naaman must obey. He has to dip in the River Jordan seven times. Please note that it *must be seven*. God means what He says. After Naaman had dipped six times, there was no change to his flesh. The leprosy was still there. He could have been discouraged and given up at the fourth or fifth dip. But Naaman is determined to *go through with God* and is healed as he comes up the *seventh time.* Just as that one last digit on the phone triggered an alarm to the police, that one last dip of obedience was the trigger which brought about healing.

If you want to *go through with God*, obedience matters. (Not a slavish, legalistic obedience, but one that is based on love). Jesus said that if we love Him, we will keep His commandments (John 14:15). We often emphasise that God is a rewarder of faith, but He also rewards obedience. *'Blessed are they that hear the Word of God, and keep it'* (Luke 11:28).

DAY 94

I Know

And he returned to the man of God, he and all his company,
and came, and stood before him: and he said,
Behold, now I know that there is no God in all the earth, but in Israel:
now therefore, I pray you, take a blessing of your servant.
2nd Kings 5:15

I don't like electric toothbrushes and rarely use them. But one night, Karis wanted to use Di's electric toothbrush. I applied the toothpaste and switched on the toothbrush. As it whirred round and round, the toothpaste went everywhere: over me, Karis' face, pyjamas and her toy panda. I eventually got it into her mouth. As I left the room, I heard my (at the time) five-year-old instruct me, *'Daddy, you put it in your mouth first, and then switch it on.'* I was taught how to use an electric toothbrush by my five-year-old child. I *thought* I could use it, but she *knew* how to use it.

Naaman has made incredible progress. In verse 11, he said, *'I thought.'* Here, in verse 15, he says, *'I know.'* His perceptions about God change entirely. Now he knows there is only one God in the Earth. The little Hebrew slave had witnessed to Naaman about the power of her God. Elisha (through his servant) told him what awaited if he would *go through with God.* But the change in Naaman's life would only come as he experienced the living God for himself through obedience and faith. It is great to hear other people tell amazing stories of what God has done in their lives, but these stories won't do us much good unless they inspire us to experience God for ourselves and step out in faith and obedience.

Before you were saved, you lived your life based on what *you thought.* Now, you live your life based on what *you know* from the Word of God. You *know* that you have eternal life (1st John 5:13). You *know* God works all things together for good to them that love Him (Romans 8:28). You *know* Whom you have believed and that He is able to keep what you have committed to Him (2nd Timothy 1:12). Encourage yourself today in what you *know* from God's Word, rather than what you *think.*

DAY 95

We Aren't There Yet

And Naaman said, Shall there not then, I pray you, be given to your servant two mules' burden of earth? for your servant will hereafter offer neither burnt offering nor sacrifice to other gods, but to the LORD.
2nd Kings 5:17

When we were young and going on a long car journey, I would have asked the same three questions. *'Do you know the way?' 'Is there enough petrol to take us there?'* And then, as the journey progressed, the last question was asked on a loop (or it must have seemed that way to my Granny who was driving): *'Are we there yet?'* I see a spiritual equivalent to those three questions. We know the way (Jesus). God has given us the power we need for the journey (through the Holy Spirit). But we aren't there yet. God has begun a work in us and will complete it one day (Philippians 1:6), but we aren't there yet. We are still on a journey. Maybe we would be more patient and forgiving with one another if we remembered that none of us have *arrived* yet. We are all still learning.

Naaman was on a journey, too. He fumbled his way through. He made mistakes. But he got there. He didn't get there alone. The Hebrew girl, Elisha and Naaman's servants all played a part in his faith journey. If you see someone stumbling along the way and making mistakes, why not walk alongside them in their journey? Unfortunately, it's easier to reach out a tongue to criticise than reach out a hand to pick someone up. Be revolutionary, *go through with God*, go against the flow and help someone along.

Naaman persevered and received the blessing of healing. Notice, however, that *going through with God* is not a one-off decision. It is a daily one. Jesus said to take up our cross daily and follow Him (Luke 9:23). Naaman will continue on with God and says he will sacrifice to no other 'gods' but the Lord. It wouldn't be easy in Gentile, idol-worshipping Syria, but Naaman was now sold out for God. Despite the unbelief around you, take up your cross daily (with the help of the Holy Spirit) and keep following Jesus.

DAY 96

Black Spots

But Gehazi, the servant of Elisha the man of God, said, Behold, my master has spared Naaman this Syrian, in not receiving at his hands that which he brought: but, as the LORD lives, I will run after him, and take somewhat of him.
2nd Kings 5:20

While driving in Southern Ireland, you may come across a road sign that lets you know you are going through an accident black spot (a place where, historically, accidents occur more frequently than in other areas). It is hoped that drivers will be careful and not experience the misfortune of others. In the Bible, we come across what we might call spiritual black spots. We are told of serious mistakes or sins others have made so we may learn from them and not go down the same path. Instead of concluding on the high point of Naaman's healing, this chapter has a sad ending of which we should take heed.

Naaman offered money to Elisha, which he refused. Gehazi saw an opportunity and came to Naaman, claiming he was collecting for two prophets who needed help. Naaman gave him money and clothing, but Gehazi kept them for himself. He was confronted by Elisha and struck down with leprosy. The lesson is that although Gehazi spent much time with Elisha and witnessed miracles, it was no guarantee his heart was right with God. His story is similar to Judas' story. Both had hearts overcome by a desire for money.

Service for God is not an indicator of the state of the heart. While serving God is something we should do out of love for Jesus, we can do it mechanically and neglect our hearts. How do we guard against this? In Nehemiah 4:17, as the wall was being rebuilt, the workers used one hand to work and the other to hold a sword to guard against the enemy's attacks. Serving God requires us to be vigilant. Put on the whole armour of God, and seek the power of the Holy Spirit to keep you from day to day. What happens if you crash into a spiritual blackspot? God has mercy and hope for those who genuinely repent. But prevention is always better than cure.

SECTION 9

THE FLOATING AXE HEAD

2nd Kings 6:1-7

DAY 97

The Boundaries Of Possibility

And the sons of the prophets said to Elisha, Behold now, the place where we dwell with you is too strait for us. Let us go, we pray you, to Jordan, and take from there every man a beam, and let us make us a place there, where we may dwell. And he answered, Go you.
2nd Kings 6:1-2

Billy called round for the first time to his new girlfriend's house, and her father stood at the door. I don't know much about what was going through the father's mind as he stood there with a shotgun behind his back (just joking), but I do suspect he was thinking in terms of boundaries. *'Where are you going?' 'Will there be anyone else with you?' 'What time do you intend to bring her home?'* In all walks of life, we think in terms of boundaries.

When it comes to faith, there are *no boundaries*. As Jesus spoke to a father whose son was under demonic attack, He said, *'If you can believe, all things are possible to him that believes'* (Mark 9:23). Jesus is saying there are endless possibilities for the person who can believe. If you can expand your faith, you can extend the *boundaries of possibility*. Let me place two caveats. We can restrict the boundaries of possibility when we restrict our faith. Earlier in that story, the disciples had been unable to cast out the demon due to a lack of faith. The other restriction is that everything is subject to God's will. We cannot ask for whatever we want. But the general rule is this: believe big, don't restrict the boundaries of possibility, and leave God to decide what is best.

In chapter 6, despite the nation being in a state of spiritual decline and barrenness, the sons of the prophets have a vision to expand where they live. They are growing despite the darkness around them. As we see the state of our world today, we can be tempted to give up and ask, *'What's the point?'* In doing so, we restrict the boundaries of possibility. Are we content to stay hemmed inside the borders of our faith, or have we a desire to *go through with God*, to expand and take more ground for His Kingdom?

DAY 98

Saving For A Rainy Day

Let us go, we pray you, to Jordan, and take from there every man a beam, and let us make us a place there, where we may dwell.
2nd Kings 6:2(a)

You look at the item in the shop and then at the money in your hand. A battle begins. *'Should I, or shouldn't I? Sure, it won't do any harm, and I haven't treated myself for a while.'* You look again at your money and shock yourself as you place it back into your wallet or purse. Next thing you know, you are lodging the money in the bank. A few days later, an unexpected bill comes through the letterbox. You are glad you had taken precautions and saved up for a rainy day.

When Elijah was about to go to Heaven, he asked Elisha what he could do for him. Elisha could have asked for anything at all, but he requested a double portion of Elijah's spirit. You may remember I said that it is possible that as Elisha saw the darkness around him (and recalled how at one stage his great mentor Elijah had been so overwhelmed by the apostasy of his day), he reckoned he would need a double portion of the spirit of Elijah.

Just as you were glad that you had taken precautions (looked down the line and saved for a rainy day), I am sure that Elisha was glad he had looked ahead and asked for this double portion. It was a wise request because, despite the darkness around them, the sons of the prophets were expanding. These men sat at the feet of Elisha and learned from him (2nd Kings 4:38). This prophet who had asked for the double portion, who *went through with God* and was on fire for God, was now passing that fire on to the sons of the prophets and they were growing. When people get on fire for God, that fire can also spread to those around them.

As we look at changing laws and the departure from God in our land, we know that humanly speaking, down the line, there are many challenges ahead. Take precautions now by seeking the fire of God and seeking to be filled with the Spirit. Pray that God will spread the fire to others, too. Be wise. Be prepared.

DAY 99

Teamwork

Let us go, we pray you, to Jordan, and take from there every man a beam, and let us make us a place there, where we may dwell. And he answered, Go you.
2nd Kings 6:2

At the end of June, our church had a *Holiday Bible Club*. It was a fantastic time. There was a buzz about the place and so many positives to come away with. I have a photo of twenty-one volunteers wearing their *Donaghcloney Elim* t-shirts. As a pastor, that photo means so much to me. It speaks of teamwork. It speaks of unity. No single person could have done everything by themselves. Some were good at leading; others at doing a quiz. Some found their gifting in doing the Bible verses; others were good at keeping order! Everyone had a part to play.

As we saw yesterday, the sons of the prophets needed a bigger place to stay as they were expanding. They asked Elisha if they could go to the Jordan. Each would take a log and help to build somewhere new. They were going to do it together. Each one would play a part in the new building.

The main factor in any work of God is of course, the power of the Holy Spirit. For those who feel overwhelmed by the task ahead, we take comfort in the words of Zechariah 4:6, where the Word of the Lord came to Zerubbabel: *'Not by might, nor by power, but by My spirit, says the LORD of hosts.'* However, from the human side, we do have our part to play, and attitude is crucial. We read about the great building project in which Nehemiah was involved, and progress came because *'The people had a mind to work' (Nehemiah 4:6).* In contrast, the building project of the tower of Babel was brought into confusion when their communication was broken down through God's intervention.

As we seek to build the Kingdom of God through various means, each one of us must lift a log (as we see in today's verse). Some can lift bigger logs than others, but we all must do our part. Ask God to show you your *'log'* and *'lift it'* in His strength.

DAY 100

Dependent On God

And one said, Be content, I pray you, and go with your servants.
2nd Kings 6:3a

It was an emotional day for Dad at the beginning of his long illness when he was told he would no longer be able to drive the car. For a young man, losing his independence was a significant blow. Dad would spend most of his adult life dependent on other people. He depended on Mum to help him get ready in the mornings. For around eight years (before we had a lift installed in the house), he depended on others to carry him down the stairs. Wherever he went, Dad depended on us to push him in his wheelchair. Sometimes, we take our ability to get around and do things ourselves for granted.

The sons of the prophets have been granted permission by Elisha to build bigger. But before they do, they have one more thing to ask. They want Elisha to go with them. They feel that they cannot do this on their own. They feel dependent on his presence with them. Elisha says that he will go.

The person who *goes through with God* will feel totally dependent on Him. Moses was a mighty man of God, but in Exodus 33:15, he pleads for God not to make his people continue their journey unless His presence goes with them. If God would not go with them, everything would be pointless. The amazing thing for us today as Christians is that we don't have to plead with God to go with us. He is with us wherever we go. Paul spoke of *'Christ in you'* (Colossians 1:27). However, despite His presence with us, we must acknowledge our need of Him and dependence upon Him daily.

Most of us see dependence as a weakness, but in the spiritual world, dependence on God is our strength. In the spiritual world, self-reliance is the way down, but dependence on God is the way up. It takes courage to admit we are absolutely nothing without God. Reach out to Him today with a humble heart.

DAY 101

His Presence Makes The Difference

And he answered, I will go.
2nd Kings 6:3b

It was night-time as I wrote today's message. Ellie couldn't sleep and asked for something to drink. I said, '*Yes, go down and get some juice*' (thinking I could keep working). But, of course, she wanted me to go with her. Even with the light on, going downstairs at night can be a scary experience for a child. Having your Daddy to hold your hand makes all the difference. (I said I would go, of course).

Yesterday, we saw how the sons of the prophets depended on Elisha. They didn't want to take on this project without his presence. Elisha simply answered, *'I will go.'* His presence made all the difference. Without him, things would be uncertain. They can now start their work with confidence.

I mentioned yesterday that while Moses pleaded with God to go with the people as they journeyed (Exodus 33:15), we don't have to plead with the Lord. He is with us always. I want to look at this a little more today.

Going back to the illustration about Ellie, I have seen her go downstairs at night on her own. She crouches over and walks very timidly. When Di or I go with her, she walks with confidence. When God was moving in my heart about going into ministry, a problem for me would have been public speaking. I am, by nature, very reserved. When I was concerned about this, I was given a verse. Jeremiah 1:8 says: *'Be not afraid of their faces: for I am with you....'* His presence with us gives us confidence.

The Lord not only goes with us, but I love Deuteronomy 31:8, which tells us the Lord Himself goes *before us.* That means that He is already there before we arrive. Maybe you have to go to the doctor's surgery tomorrow. He is already there. Is it a job interview, family crisis, or sad goodbye? He is already there before you arrive. May that give you confidence and comfort today.

DAY 102

The Little Things Matter To God

But as one was felling a beam, the axe head fell into the water:
2nd Kings 6:5a

One day, as we played pitch and putt (just outside Portstewart), I swung at the ball, and the head of the golf club flew through the air at top speed. It could have been dangerous had it hit someone on the head. It reminds me of another incident when we were driving onto *Portstewart Strand*, and a golf ball crashed through the windscreen of the car in front (just missing us). Today's verse is not about a flying golf ball or golf club but a flying axe head.

The sons of the prophets go to Jordan and begin chopping trees. As one is chopping, his axe head flies off the handle and is lost. Why would the Bible record the story of a lost axe head? In the previous chapter, we have been dealing with probably the second most powerful man in Syria. We have seen a miracle take place as he is healed of leprosy. Where does an axe head come into the grand scheme of things? We shall see tomorrow that this incident is actually more serious than it seems, but let's just take it at face value today. Is God concerned with the little things in our lives? The answer is a resounding *'Yes.'* The mighty God of Heaven, Who rules this universe, holding the world together with the Word of His Power, deeply cares about the things that concern you.

While Jesus was dying on the cross and accomplishing the great work of Redemption, in the middle of all of His agony and suffering, He was concerned that someone would care for His mother. Psalm 56:8 reminds us that God cares about the tears we shed. It gives us a picture of God collecting them in a bottle and writing them in a book. Luke 12:7 tells us that the very hairs on our heads are numbered. God understands our concerns about the food we eat and the clothes we wear but assures us to put Him first, and everything else will fall into place (Matthew 6:25-34). However big or small your cares, cast them all on Jesus, for He cares for you (1st Peter 5:7).

DAY 103

When Clouds Hover Over

.....and he cried, and said, Alas, master! for it was borrowed.
2nd Kings6:5b

I am exaggerating a bit here, but sometimes I feel that I spend around fifty per cent of my life looking for things that are lost. I am sure some men can relate to this: maybe you aren't the tidiest person, and some describe your office or room as messy, but it is an *organized mess*. You know exactly where everything is. Then *'someone'* decides to tidy the mess, and from that moment onwards, you can't find a thing. You ask that *'someone'* for the location of an item you can no longer find, and *she* can`t remember where *she* moved them to (unless it was the bin)!

This passage is about something that is lost: an axe head. Yesterday, we saw that God is concerned even about the little things in our lives. But today, we will discover that this episode may have been more problematic than we first thought. You see, the axe head was borrowed.

Today, you can purchase an axe for under forty pounds sterling, but in Elisha's time, an axe head would have been very expensive. In fact, it was so costly that if Elisha's pupil could not pay the money back, it was possible that he could have been taken into slavery.[18] That's how bad the situation could have become. A dark cloud now hovers over the work they are attempting to complete. They may end up owing a lot of money. The work is at risk.

I remember times when I was determined to *go through with God*. Once I made that decision, it seemed as if opposition and problems appeared from seemingly nowhere. These things can sometimes distract and even discourage us. However, it's not so much the problems that come when you attempt to do something for God; it's what you do with those problems that counts. The sons of the prophets had already wisely invited Elisha to come with them. Jesus is already in your situation. He knows about it. Call on Him and ask Him to show you what to do. He will see you through.

DAY 104

Where Did You Lose It?

And the man of God said, Where fell it? And he showed him the place.
2nd Kings 6:6a

When someone loses something, what is the first question you ask? *'Where did you see it last?'* Did you know that something similar was asked even back in Bible times? One of the sons of the prophets swings an axe; the head flies off and lands in the water. Elisha asks, *'Where did it fall?'* In effect, he is asking where he saw it last. It's a sensible question to ask.

The whole of Luke chapter 15 speaks about three things that are lost: a lost sheep, a lost coin and a lost son. God is interested in things that are lost. Jesus' mission was to seek and to save that which was lost (Luke 19:10).

I could perhaps speak to you about a lost axe head, but my mind is directed to something more important. I wonder, have you lost ground with God? Maybe you can recall times when you set out to *go through with God*, but that all got lost somewhere along the way. You remember times of blessing when your heart burned with fire as you read His Word, prayed, and passionately served God. But something happened, and your fire has gone out. So, the question comes: *'Where did you lose it?'* Losing ground with God doesn't always happen suddenly. Mostly, it is gradual. A little bit here and a little bit there. Something gradually took a greater place in your life than God. He fell into second or third place (or even lower). Maybe it wasn't something that pushed God out, but someone. *'Where did you lose it?'*

Whether or not you can remember where you lost ground with God, the good news is that you can get back to where you were before you lost ground. In fact, the Lord can take you to higher ground than you ever were before. Peter lost ground when he denied the Lord, but when he was restored, he was filled with the Holy Spirit, and God used him to a greater extent than ever before. *Go through with God again.* Give Him first place in your life, and watch how he restores the ground you had lost.

DAY 105

Iron Axe Heads Don't Float - Except....

And he cut down a stick, and cast it in there; and the iron did swim.
2nd Kings 6:6b

Dad had to get a heart valve replaced at the age of thirty-one. It was in 1971, and there were not the same medical advancements then as compared to today. It was a massive operation, and Mum and Dad were told of the risks. Mum was advised to go home and get some rest as it would be a long operation. Later, the phone rang from the hospital, and Mum was urgently told to come as soon as possible. Before leaving, my Grandmother phoned Peggy Emerson, an amazing lady and good friend of the family. She had been told of the potential risks and had a list of names ready to phone to ask for prayer if needed. As Mum and Granny left for the hospital, Peggy made the calls and prayer was made for Dad. After the operation, the surgeon spoke with Mum. He told her that Dad had begun bleeding during surgery. They kept giving him more blood, but he continued to bleed. There seemed to be no end to it, and things looked hopeless. But suddenly, Dad stopped bleeding. The surgeon said he had never seen anything like it before. Although he was an agnostic, he did say that if a God existed, then a miracle had just taken place. Mum witnessed to him that day about the power of prayer.

A borrowed axe head had been lost in water and could be costly to replace. Elisha cut a stick, threw it into the water, and the iron axe head began to float. They had found it at last. But wait. Iron doesn't float - except when the power of God is involved. Surgeons see things they have never witnessed before when the power of God is involved. Can I encourage you today? Prodigals don't suddenly come home - except when the power of God is involved. Friends and family seem disinterested in Jesus - except when the power of God is involved. Those mountains in your life never seem to move - except when the power of God is involved. When God moves in a situation, the impossible becomes possible. He is still the God of miracles.

DAY 106

Grabbing An Opportunity With Both Hands

Therefore said he, Take it up to you.
And he put out his hand, and took it.
2nd Kings 2:7

When I was almost drowning in a lake in Switzerland, I came to the surface and saw my cousin's hand reaching out. I took my opportunity, grabbed that hand and was rescued. One evening, down on one knee, I proposed to Di. I was determined to take the opportunity to ask her to be my wife. I wasn't going to let her get away! A couple of years later, we took out a mortgage on a house which had dropped in price by around fifty per cent due to a recent bank and housing crash. We weren't going to miss out on such a good deal. These three events were opportunities which, to use a saying, I *'grabbed with both hands.'*

As we conclude this section, the sons of the prophets have hit some trouble as a borrowed axe head has been lost. There would be the possibility that if they couldn`t pay back the money, one of their number may have to go into slavery. When, through the power of God, the iron axe head miraculously floats on the water, Elisha says to take it. We read that his pupil put out his hand and took it. You can imagine that when he took the axe head, he grabbed it with both hands and wouldn't let it go. He wasn't going to miss his opportunity. He didn't want to be sold into slavery.

Ephesians 5:16 instructs us to redeem the time (which really means to make the most of every opportunity).[19] Today, opportunities will undoubtedly come our way, through which we can make a difference for the Kingdom of God. It could be through coming alongside someone and giving a listening ear, doing a kind deed, speaking a word of influence or praying. The possibilities are endless. Whether we take these opportunities or not may depend on how much they mean to us. Are we laid-back about these opportunities, or do we have the passion and fire to grab them with both hands? Today's unique opportunity may just help to change someone's future forever.

SECTION 10

WHO IS SURROUNDING WHOM?

2nd Kings 6:8-23

DAY 107

What Does The Future Hold?

And the man of God sent to the king of Israel, saying, Beware that you pass not such a place; for there the Syrians are come down.
2nd Kings 6:9

My wife, Di, heard a story about a woman who claimed to be a clairvoyant. She stopped someone and said, *'Put some money in my palm, and I will tell you your future.'* She asked the wrong person because they took out a Bible and said, *'I will tell you your future for free!'* The person went on to say that if this clairvoyant kept going as she was, her future would be a lost one without Jesus. I assume this person also told her the good news that Jesus could set her free.

The king of Syria was attacking Israel. Whenever he made plans to camp his armies in a particular place, the word always got back to the king of Israel with this information. If that happened today, there would be a massive spy scandal on the Syrian news channels. Who is leaking this sensitive war information to Israel? You can imagine the stir it caused. The king of Syria thinks he has a traitor among his people, but word somehow gets to one of his servants that Elisha is providing this information. Elisha is hearing from God. The king gives the command to go and capture Elisha.

You might say to yourself that it would be great if we could know what will happen tomorrow, or have some supernatural insight about things that are happening around us. God has always revealed hidden things to His people throughout history, and He still does today. But generally, we are called to walk daily, not knowing exactly what lies ahead. Paul said that we walk by faith and not by sight (2nd Corinthians 5:7). Abraham was called to leave the land of Ur, and he didn't even know his destination. But Hebrews 11:8 says that he went by faith.

I love Psalm 77:20, which tells us that the Lord led His people like a flock by the hand of Moses and Aaron. The way ahead may seem dark, but more important than knowing the path before us is knowing the Shepherd, and He knows what lies ahead.

DAY 108

Hearing From Headquarters

And one of his servants said, None, my lord, O king: but Elisha,
the prophet that is in Israel, tells the king of Israel
the words that you speak in your bedchamber.
2nd Kings 6:12

You have heard the expression, *'Oh, to be a fly on the wall in that conversation.'* Elisha could tell the very words the king of Syria spoke in private. Elisha wasn't standing in the adjoining room with his ear to a glass placed against the wall, but was hearing from God. It is timely to remind ourselves that God is the silent listener to every conversation. He knows the very thoughts and motives of our hearts. God knew the hearts of Ananias and Sapphira as they kept back money for themselves. Jesus knew that Judas was going to betray Him. God had supernaturally revealed to Elisha that Gehazi had taken money from Naaman and hidden it for himself.

God does not change (Malachi 3:6; Hebrews 13:8) and still speaks to His people today. C.H. Spurgeon's autobiography[20] tells how, on one occasion, while preaching, he announced there was a man in the meeting who had traded illegally on a Sunday (it was against the law back then). He then revealed how much money the man had taken, along with his exact profit. The man was astounded at how Spurgeon knew and also by his accuracy. He realised that God had spoken through the preacher and subsequently got saved.

In a war, headquarters needs to communicate with the soldiers on the ground and also (through the use of intelligence) find out what the enemy is doing. As we fight the Christian battle, seeking to *go through with God*, it is comforting to know that God still communicates with His people today. It gives us confidence when we understand that He knows the enemy's strategies precisely. The Lord is always many steps ahead of our adversaries and is never taken by surprise. Rather than being fearful of what the enemy has up his sleeve, trust the God Who knows the end from the beginning. *And keep those communication lines open.*

DAY 109

The Wee Small Hours

Therefore sent he there horses, and chariots, and a great host: and they came by night, and compassed the city about.
2nd Kings 6:14

My Grandmother routinely woke in the middle of the night and began to go over things in her mind. I gave her a little hint by buying a small plaque to put by her bed, which advised that when you can't sleep, instead of counting sheep, talking to the Shepherd was a better idea! After pondering everything, she would shout, *'Lorna!'* (my Mum) *'Can you get me some tea and toast?'* Then, she would discuss everything that had been going through her head with Mum. This scenario was repeated time after time.

The king of Syria has discovered that Elisha is hearing from God and divulging his plans to the king of Israel. He decides that his best plan of action is to capture Elisha. This was perhaps not his brightest idea, as God could easily reveal His plans to another prophet. The king sends a great army along with horses and chariots. But notice that he sends them at night. In warfare, the dark hours of night have traditionally been an excellent time to attack the enemy. It holds the element of surprise, and the night hours can instil fear through being unable to see the enemy.

In the night hours, we can so often experience spiritual attacks. We remember things that have happened during the day or perhaps anxiously fear tomorrow. Psalm 91:5 reminds us that when we trust in the Lord and hide in Him, we will not be afraid of the terror by night. Psalm 16:7 reminds us that God can advise us in the night hours. The Psalmist meditated on God during the night (Psalm 63:6). Job 35:10 speaks of God giving His people songs at night. When the enemy attacks in the *'wee small hours,'* meditate on God, hide in Him, and listen for His voice as He instructs you. Allow redemption songs to fill your soul. Psalm 127:2 tells us that God gives His loved ones sleep. I believe that sleep can come when we focus entirely on Him.

DAY 110

When You Feel Hemmed In

And when the servant of the man of God was risen early, and gone forth, behold, a host compassed the city both with horses and chariots.
2nd Kings 6:15a

I will never live it down. I was using our childhood pet budgie as part of a sermon illustration. I said something like this: *'One morning, we came downstairs and found Peter* (the budgie) *lying on his back with his four feet in the air!'* I didn't realise what I had said. Looking down across both sides of the church, I could see smiles but couldn't figure out why. After the service, all was made plain! I wonder what it must feel for a bird trapped inside a cage. Its natural environment is flying freely in the open space, yet it is surrounded by bars inside a metal cage.

The king of Syria has ordered that Elisha should be captured, and now the city is surrounded by his army. Elisha and his servant are trapped with nowhere to go. Life can be like that sometimes. We can feel caged up, trapped, surrounded, and hemmed in. It seems there is no way out.

We can recall how Jesus, too, was surrounded. In Psalm 22, David prophetically describes the scene around the cross. As the crowd mocked and scorned the Saviour, verse 12 speaks allegorically of Jesus being surrounded by strong bulls of Bashan. You can see the picture of large bulls encircling with horns ready to attack. That is how it felt for Jesus on the cross. Jesus knows how you feel when it seems everything is closing in on you. He can enter into that situation with you.

As Jesus faced the surrounding evil forces, He did it alone. He cried out to His Father, *'Why have you forsaken Me?'* (Psalm 22:1; Matthew 27:46). He did so to save us from our sins. Because He faced the enemy alone on the cross and won the battle, whenever we feel surrounded by the forces of evil, we don't go through it alone. Hell's surrounding forces could not defeat Jesus on that cross, and though they may encircle you today, you are completely safe as you hide in the victorious Saviour.

DAY 111

When All Hope Seems Gone

And his servant said to him,
Alas, my master! how shall we do?
2nd Kings 6:15b

Geordie would have told you himself that he was a *rough diamond* in his time, but now, praise God, he was saved. He was also one of life's characters. Geordie had been told he had an aneurysm. He could live for years, or it could do its damage at any time. The church family was in Newcastle for a day out when I got the news that Geordie had taken ill and was in hospital. As I arrived there, he told me, *'Pastor, they have said I'm on my way out. There's nothing they can do.'* I couldn't take it in because he was sitting up and talking away to everyone. He added, *'But Pastor, I'm not afraid to die. I'm ready to go.'* Before I left, I prayed, and then we sang, *'Jesus loves me.'* [21] It would have taken a tear from a stone to hear that former rough diamond sing along. The next day, Geordie's situation had deteriorated. He was in and out of sleep. At one stage, he gave me his hand. I joked, *'Geordie, this isn't Maureen* (his wife), *it's the Pastor.'* He softly said, *'I know!'* Geordie went to be with the Lord later that night.

The Syrian army surrounded Elisha and his servant. Things weren't looking good, and it seemed like the end. As I read how Elisha's servant asked what they would do, my mind turned to Geordie. What do you do when the doctors say they cannot help you? What do you do when your back is against the wall? What do you do when all seems hopeless? For Christians, when everything is stripped away, and nothing is left, we still have Jesus. What Geordie did was to have confidence in the hope that Jesus Christ gave him when all other hope was gone. Geordie left this world with the confident knowledge of where he was going.

What can you do when all hope seems gone? You can rest in the *living hope* that Peter speaks of (1st Peter 1:3). Because He lives, we shall live also (see John 14:19). If you are reading these words and don't know Jesus, be sure to call on Him today for salvation.

DAY 112

Paralysed With Fear

And he answered, Fear not:
2nd Kings 6:16a

This year, we went to the amusements in Portrush. There was a new ride which replaced the *'Big Dipper.'* It takes you up a steep gradient, and then you suddenly fall sharply down a high drop towards some water. Both kids wanted to go on it, but during the first ride, Ellie cried, Karis cried, and I almost cried! They were screaming and wanted off, but it was too late by then, as it went up the second time. When you know what is coming, you are even more scared. They were almost *paralysed with fear.*

As we saw yesterday, the Syrian army surrounded Elisha and his servant. It seemed that there was no hope. Elisha's servant was *paralysed with fear.*

Our faith can suffer when we are overcome by fear. It attacks our assurance and confidence in God. Fear takes our eyes off how great our God is and focuses on how great our problem is. Next, our peace will be affected. Peace and fear cannot walk in harmony. Fear disturbs our peace. Then, as we allow fear to take over our hearts, we will find our joy begins to fade. How can our joy be full when we are filled with fear instead? Here, we have one arrow of fear attacking at least three major areas of our spiritual lives: assurance, peace and joy. Therefore, Elisha's words to his servant are also vital for us today. *'Fear not.'* Don't allow this arrow of fear to cause damage to your spirit.

It is essential to understand where fear *does not* come from. Paul writes that God has not given us the spirit of fear. But there is something that He does want to impart to us: a spirit of power, love and a sound mind (2nd Timothy 1:7). John says that perfect (or complete) love casts out fear (1st John 4:18). How do we cultivate a less fearful heart? When we ask the Holy Spirit to transform us. *Going through with God* will involve a deeper walk in the Spirit as we lay our hearts open before Him and surrender to His ways. *'The fruit of the Spirit is love, joy, peace……'* (Galatians 5:22, 23).

DAY 113

Good Reasons Not To Fear

And he answered, Fear not: for they that be with us are more than they that be with them.
2nd Kings 6:16

Ellie asked Karis, *'Who is your superhero?'* I interrupted and answered on her behalf: *'Her Daddy.'* Ellie immediately replied, *'Daddy, you're not a superhero; you're a pastor!'* I know there's a message in there somewhere, but I just can't figure out what it is yet! The Syrian army surrounds Elisha and his servant. It is just two men against a whole army. They don't stand a chance, humanly speaking. Yet, Elisha tells his servant not to fear. What is he talking about? Elisha is only a prophet, only a man. He isn't some sort of superhero in a cape. Surely, they have every right to be afraid?

When you tell someone not to be afraid, it is best to have a good reason to give to them; otherwise, it defeats the purpose. Elisha tells his servant not to be afraid and then gives the reason. It is because there are more on their side than the enemy. We shall look more at that aspect tomorrow, but let's concentrate today on how God's Word gives us good reasons not to be afraid.

Isaiah 43:1 instructs us not to fear because *God has redeemed us*. This is the principal reason why we should not fear. Jesus has set us free through what He has done on Calvary. We have been brought into the family of God. In this verse, the Lord also says that we *belong to Him*. In Psalm 23:4, we need not fear even if it's the valley of the shadow of death because our Shepherd is *with us* every step of the way. In Deuteronomy 3:22, we should not be afraid because *the Lord fights for us*. Psalm 46:1-3 encourages us not to fear even in the most cataclysmic circumstances because *God is our refuge and strength* when troubles come. Jesus said not to let our hearts be troubled because *He has left us with His peace* (John 14:27). Search for the phrases *'Fear not'* and *'Be not afraid'* and list the reasons given why we should not fear. You will be greatly encouraged. But don't forget to put it into practice!

DAY 114

What You See Is What You Get

And Elisha prayed, and said, LORD, I pray you, open his eyes, that he may see. And the LORD opened the eyes of the young man; and he saw: and, behold, the mountain was full of horses and chariots of fire round about Elisha.
2nd Kings 6:17

The traffic lights had turned green. I drove forward and turned towards the left. At that point, another car came at high speed from my right-hand side (from seemingly nowhere). He went through the red lights, slammed on his brakes and stopped literally a few centimetres away from my driver's door. I have never come as close to being involved in a major accident. It was definitely the grace of God that protected me that day. I was aware that the traffic lights on my side were green. He was unaware that the traffic lights on his side were red. We both saw two completely different things that day, which almost had considerable consequences.

In this passage, Elisha and his servant see two completely different things. And what they see makes all the difference to how they are reacting. Elisha's servant sees a Syrian army surrounding the city. Elisha sees a Heavenly army in the mountains surrounding him. Elisha's servant was paralysed by fear. Elisha was at peace. What you see will determine how you will react.

The army of Israel, along with King Saul, could see a massive giant called Goliath. Their reaction was fear. A young man named David came along. Physically, he saw exactly the same as the others, but spiritually, he saw something else. He saw, by faith, a God Who was bigger than any giant. What he saw by faith gave him the courage to take on Goliath in the Name of the Lord.

You have heard the expression, *'What you see is what you get.'* And it is true in the battle of faith. If all we can see is what is in front of our eyes, then our reactions will be based on what we see. But if we can look past what we physically see and into the spiritual realm, we can find the courage to *go through with God.*

DAY 115

Lovingly Surrounded

.....and he saw: and, behold, the mountain was full of horses and chariots of fire round about Elisha.
2nd Kings 6:17b

If I go online and zoom into a map of Northern Ireland, it seems to be quite big as I look around its towns and villages. When I zoom out, I see our little country surrounded by a vast world that makes us look so small. But then, if I zoom out further and look at planet Earth, it is surrounded by a vast universe and looks like a little ball. It's all about perspective. As Elisha's servant looks with his physical eyes, all he can see is a massive Syrian army surrounding the city. But Elisha sees from a different perspective. He can see a Heavenly army in the mountains surrounding himself. Yes, they are surrounded, but ultimately, *God surrounds them*. To get to Elisha, the Syrians first have to go through a Heavenly army, which will not happen. I want to remind you today that God surrounds you, no matter how hemmed in you feel by life's circumstances. You are under His protection. Let's have a look at how lovingly you are surrounded.

God is watching over you. Psalm 32:8 says, 'I will instruct you and teach you in the way which you shall go: I will guide you with My eye.' **God is beneath you, holding you up.** We read in Deuteronomy 33:27: 'The eternal God is your refuge, and underneath are the everlasting arms:' **God's goodness is following you from behind.** 'Surely goodness and mercy shall follow me all the days of my life:' (Psalm 23:6). **God leads the way in front of you.** 'And the LORD, He it is that does go before you; He will be with you, He will not fail you, neither forsake you: fear not, neither be dismayed.' (Deuteronomy 31:8). **God surrounds you like a mountain.** 'As the mountains are round about Jerusalem, so the LORD is round about His people from hereafter even forever' (Psalm 125:2).

Let's get the proper perspective and 'zoom out' to see a mighty God surrounding His people. You are in His care. Fear not.

DAY 116

A Revolutionary Way Of Living

And he prepared great provision for them: and when they had eaten and drunk, he sent them away, and they went to their master. So the bands of Syria came no more into the land of Israel.
2nd Kings 6:23

The conclusion of this story is unexpected. Elisha prays for God to strike the Syrian army with blindness, and he leads them right into the presence of the king of Israel. He then prays that their eyes would be opened. The king had never expected this and excitedly asks if he should kill them. Elisha answers that it would be wrong. He says to give them food and water and let them go. Due to this act of compassion, the Syrians ditched their policy of making terror raids into Israel.

What Elisha did was not normal. The natural instinct would be to punish your enemies. The person who wants to *go through with God* will be confronted with similar scenarios. Sometimes, the flesh screams out for revenge, but the Holy Spirit whispers mercy and grace. Which course of action will we take?

Going through with God is revolutionary. Jesus said to bless those who curse you and pray for those who mistreat you (Luke 6:28). This was not just a cold, rigid instruction, but something that Jesus practised Himself, even while on the cross. Think of the vile insults sinners hurled at the Son of God as He hung there, bearing our sins. With a heart of love, Jesus prayed, 'Father, forgive them, for they know not what they do' (Luke 23:34). We may be tempted to think, *'That was Jesus, He is God. He is perfect. I could not be so radical in forgiving those who hurt me.'* While Stephen was being martyred, he cried to God that He would not lay this sin to their account (Acts 7:60). Stephen was just an ordinary person like you and me, but he allowed the Holy Spirit to work on his heart and transform him. If God can do that to Stephen, He can do it to us also, but we must allow Him. The remarkable testimony of Stephen was that as he died, He was *full of the Holy Ghost*. (Acts 7:55). What a way to go!

SECTION 11

TIME TO GET UP AND MOVE

2nd Kings 7:1-20

DAY 117

Intensified Anticipation

Then Elisha said, Hear you the word of the LORD;
2nd Kings 7:1a

Every parent must fear those frightening teenage years. It's the age when their precious child is overcome with delusions of grandeur and thinks they know it all! Not always, but sometimes, the later teenage years can turn into rebellion against Christian parents and that young person makes their way into the big wide world. For some, it has been the case that, over time, things have become really tough, and as they sit alone at night, they long for a parent's voice again. They long for words of advice which before they had shunned. They long for a listening ear and an arm around the shoulder, telling them all will be OK. As the prodigal sat in that pigsty, he would have loved to have heard his father's voice one more time.

The story of Israel is complex. They were recipients of the love of Almighty God. At times, they responded to that love but often went astray. As God called them back, they returned for a time but soon went back to their old ways. God then had to use more severe means to bring them to repentance, which again worked for a time, but they would backslide once more. And the cycle went on. Yet throughout the rebellion and stubbornness of the nation, the faithful voice of God echoed through the centuries of time. Though they have broken His heart time and time again, He still calls in mercy and grace.

In this passage, Israel is in trouble again. It is a seven-year famine. As we saw before, famine came when the nation was unfaithful to God. Added to that, they were under siege. Yet in the middle of it all, we read, *'Hear....the Word of the Lord.'* What a faithful God. There are times when we aren't spiritually in the place we know we should be. Maybe we haven't necessarily backslidden, but we aren't giving God the place He deserves. Through all the noise and distractions in our lives, a voice is calling us to *hear the Word of the Lord.* Will we respond to that voice today?

DAY 118

Speak It Out

Then Elisha said, Hear you the word of the LORD;
Thus says the LORD, Tomorrow about this time shall a measure of fine flour be sold for a shekel, and two measures of barley for a shekel, in the gate of Samaria
2nd Kings 7:1

Writing a devotional (or any book) can be exciting but also draining. There is a lot of work involved and burning of the midnight oil. Sometimes, when the pressure gets too much, you are tempted to ask if it is worth the hard work. Today, I received a phone call from a long-time friend of Mum and Dad, who told me how much he had enjoyed my first devotional book, *'Just A Moment.'* That may not seem much to anyone else, but it was such an encouragement to me. It just gave me the lift which I needed. The thing is that even though he had been blessed by the book, something within him felt that he should phone me. He somehow got my number, and called.

Israel is suffering from a seven-year famine and is also under siege. Things could not get much worse. The Word of the Lord came to Elisha that the next day, prices would be outlandishly low (so cheap it was almost impossible, especially during a famine). All they had to do was hold on. As incredible as this Word was, God had given him Words of comfort, *and he spoke them.* It doesn't sound like a big thing to do, but what hope it brought to hopeless hearts. No one else had been given that particular Word except Elisha. It was up to him to speak it. What a privilege.

Has God given you words of comfort or encouragement to speak to someone? Has He put something upon your heart, and you know it is for a specific person? We can feel awkward about these things, but those particular words may be just what that person needs today. There may be no one else who will encourage them but you. What a privilege that God has put it on your heart to speak for Him. Don't put it off. *Go through with God,* and the Holy Spirit will give you the help needed to speak those words today.

DAY 119

Mercy Is Available

Then Elisha said, Hear you the word of the LORD;
Thus says the LORD, Tomorrow about this time shall a measure of fine flour be sold for a shekel, and two measures of barley for a shekel, in the gate of Samaria
2nd Kings 7:1

I was in Switzerland at the time and had been brought to a BBQ. There was plenty of meat on the go. There were long carved wooden sticks (almost like lances), and you would stick them in the meat and hold them over the fire to cook. I was asked if I would like a particular piece of meat. I'm glad I inquired what type of meat it was because it turned out to be horse meat! I politely refused. Just a few moments later, a horse came trotting past along with its rider. I hope they weren't eating its cousin!

Due to the famine and siege, things were so bad that people were eating donkeys' heads (2nd Kings 6:25). They ate worse than that, but I will spare the details in case you are eating while reading this book. Just as the prodigal son had been brought so low that he would almost have eaten the pigs' food, so prodigal Israel was reduced to eating donkeys' heads, which were unclean for them. Sin reduces us to do things we never would have dreamed of.

Often, the prophets would have come with a Word of judgment to Israel, but as we saw yesterday, Elisha came with a W*ord of comfort and mercy from God. In* Habakkuk 3:2, the prophet cries out for God to remember mercy in the middle of His wrath. I want to remind you there is mercy with the Lord. He is not willing that any should perish, but that all should repent (see 2nd Peter 3:9).

Maybe you have wandered from God. Perhaps you feel as if you are experiencing a spiritual famine in your life. It feels like you are besieged by guilt, anxiety and life's problems. There is One Who waits to show you mercy. There is no mercy like God's mercy. Grace is getting what we *don't deserve*. Mercy is not receiving what we *do deserve*. You can have both right now by simply calling on the powerful Name of Jesus.

DAY 120

Unbelief Holds Back Blessing

Then a lord on whose hand the king leaned answered the man of God, and said, Behold, if the LORD would make windows in heaven, might this thing be? And he said, Behold, you shall see it with your eyes, but shall not eat thereof.
2nd Kings 7:2

Suppose I told you that tomorrow petrol would be fifty-five pence per litre. (Petrol prices haven't been that low since around the mid-1990s).[22] Would you believe me? Answers on a postcard. Now, suppose the Prime Minister stands outside Downing Street, announcing the same message. While you may think it is almost impossible, you would be inclined to believe him because he told it to the nation using *his authority* as Prime Minister. I hadn't the authority to say it, but he did.

Elisha has said something just as incredible as announcing that petrol would be fifty-five pence per litre. Inflation is sky-high in the city, and prices have gone through the roof. Prices are determined partly by supply levels, and no supplies are coming through due to the siege and the famine. It seemed ridiculous when Elisha announced that prices would be so low the next day. But he made this proclamation with *his authority as a prophet of God and in the Name of the Lord.* A man (a right-hand man to the king) who doubted Elisha's message was present. He questioned the authority, not only of the prophet but *subsequently of God.*

We know God rewards faith, but this story reminds us that unbelief holds back the blessing. Hebrews 3:16 speaks of those who could not enter the Promised Land due to their unbelief. Elisha told the king's right-hand man that he would not get to enjoy the blessing because of his unbelief. Unbelief calls God a liar. Unbelief is a thief. It is a discourager. Unbelief makes us anxious and fills the heart with fear and confusion. What is the antidote to unbelief? Faith comes by hearing, and hearing by the Word of God (Romans 10:17). Immerse yourself in the Bible. Unbelief will run for the hills when you stand on the authority of God's Word.

DAY 121

The Invisible Men

And there were four leprous men at the entering in of the gate:
2nd Kings 7:3a

In Bible times, if lepers had not been required to call out, *'Unclean, unclean!'* they would have been almost invisible. To most people, they might as well be dead. Although the physical aspect of leprosy was terrible enough, the emotional fallout must have been mentally excruciating. Thankfully, the medical advancements against this awful disease have been remarkable. In this passage, we will find that four men who are literally invisible to the rest of society are not invisible to God. The Lord sees the marginalised of society. God knows those who are ostracised by others. He hears the cries and sees the tears of the lonely.

One of the most fascinating verses about Jesus' healing ministry is found in Matthew 8:3, where it is recorded that Jesus reached out His hand and touched a leper. We would normally just read past that, as we use the feeling of touch daily. But for probably years, no one had touched this poor, almost invisible man. You can practically hear the onlookers gasp as Jesus dares to touch someone unclean. What must it have been like to be Divinely touched by the One Who is love personified?

I want you also to see that these four lepers are going to be used by God to bring the message of blessing to the rest of the city. Surely this shouldn't be in the script? Surely the king should discover the food, or why not the prophet Elisha? It seems that God almost delights in using those everyone else writes off. This is a God Who can even use a donkey to speak His Word to a wayward prophet (Numbers 22:28). Many people are sitting in churches (and outside of them) who feel as if they are invisible. They feel like a *nobody*. They think they do not have the skills, talents or 'charisma' to be used for God's glory. For this reason alone, they are probably more qualified than most because that's who God tends to choose. Why not go along and encourage someone who is feeling invisible today?

DAY 122

Weighing Things Up

And there were four leprous men at the entering in of the gate: and they said one to another, Why sit we here until we die?
2nd Kings 7:3

Should we go on the cable car or not? Di and I had to weigh things up. I had been on cable cars before in Switzerland, but they were usually sturdy ones that held several people. This one in Spain looked very flimsy and was only for two people. We decided to try it. Wrong decision! As we went up towards the mountain, the cable car stopped. I assume it was to let us see the view. There was a light wind, and we were stranded there, swaying from side to side. Things got so bad that I started to recite, *'The Lord is my Shepherd, I shall not want!'* etc. Di still laughs at me doing that, but I couldn't wait to get back on solid ground.

We weighed things up and made the wrong decision. We didn't factor in on the wind. The four lepers come to the city gate, where the Syrian army is camped inside. They weigh things up. Do they stay outside and die of starvation, or go inside, where they may be killed anyway? They decide to take their chances regardless and try to get in. In Luke 14, Jesus spoke about *weighing things up*. He pointed out how crazy it would be for someone to build a tower without first weighing up if he had enough materials to finish it. Likewise, the king going to war would be foolish not to weigh up if it was wise to fight against someone with vastly more soldiers.

We weigh things up every day in life. It's a good thing to do. Jesus said that it is vital to weigh things up spiritually. In Luke 14, He was speaking in the context of family. Family is so important, but do you value Jesus more than your family, friends, business or entertainment? Many people will sit down and scrutinise their bank account (which, of course, is essential) but never examine their spiritual lives. Have you weighed things up? Which is more important to you: the spiritual or the temporal? It's a wise person Who builds their foundation on Jesus. He is the solid Rock on which we can stand for eternity.

DAY 123

Chancers

And there were four leprous men at the entering in of the gate: and they said one to another, Why sit we here until we die?
2nd Kings 7:3

We are all *'chancers'* to some extent. I'm not using the word here negatively (such as a charlatan), but we do take chances and seize on opportunities for our own good. Our kids can be *'chancers.'* They wanted to stay up late one night to play. I said *'No.'* Karis came a few moments later and looked at me with those big brown eyes. *'Please, Daddy? Just a few more minutes.'* I conceded. *'Just for a couple of minutes.'* She walked away in victory, and I heard her say to Ellie, *'We've got a few more minutes. I put on my 'please' face.'* I was taken in by my (at the time) six-year-old daughter. She is a little *'chancer'* if ever I saw one (she was just being cute; they are great kids).

These lepers realise they will die of starvation if they stay where they are. They would most likely die if they went into the enemy's camp, but it was worth having a go. It was worth taking the chance. It was an opportunity they had to take. I want to examine their question: *'Why do we sit here until we die?'*

I understand this is a devotional book mainly for Christians, but perhaps this book is in your hands, and you are not a Christian. Maybe you have thought about coming to Jesus for salvation but keep putting it off. What would your friends say? How would you keep salvation? (You don't keep it; He keeps you). One thing is sure: *if you stay where you are, you will be lost without Jesus.* You have this moment now to weigh things up as the lepers did and to take your opportunity. Your soul is worth so much. You have nothing to lose and so much to gain.

Maybe you are a backslider. You are missing out with God. If you stay where you are, you can never truly be happy away from Jesus. As with the lepers, ask yourself, *'Why should I sit here?'* Get up and *go through with God.* Your Father waits for you with loving arms. Seize this opportunity right now, and just *come home.*

DAY 124

Motivated To Find A Solution

And they rose up in the twilight, to go to the camp of the Syrians: and when they were come to the uttermost part of the camp of Syria, behold, there was no man there.
2nd Kings 7:5

I previously told you about being in hospital due to an inflamed appendix. The first time I had the pain, I was literally walking the floorboards. It was excruciating, and I could get no ease. The night hours seem to make things worse when you cannot sleep. At the time, I was the only person in the house and decided I needed to get to a hospital. The drive seemed to take forever, and once I arrived, I found out that the *Accident and Emergency* section had closed down recently. I got back into the car, still in a lot of pain and made my way to the next hospital. I was there for a couple of hours when the pain left completely. After all that! They sent me home, but I was back a couple of months later, and this time, they removed the appendix.

The lepers decided they weren't going to sit there until they died, so they *'rose up.'* Just as my problem (the pain) was the incentive that sent me looking for a solution (the hospital), the lepers' problem (hunger) was what motivated them to get up and move. It was in doing so they found their solution (food).

None of us like problems, but often, they motivate us to seek a solution. The prodigal had a big problem, being at rock bottom. But when he was at his lowest, he developed a hunger for home (which he probably never had when enjoying the supposed good times in the far country). Now, with everything else stripped away in his life, we read in Luke 15:20, *'He arose.'* His problem was what activated his desire to go home. We all have problems in our lives. No one is immune. But perhaps those problems have been motivating you to *rise up* like the lepers and the prodigal and seek the solution. Maybe those problems have propelled you in the direction of your Heavenly Father. *Go through with God.* Run to Jesus. He is the only answer.

DAY 125

Preparing To Take A Risk

And they rose up in the twilight, to go unto the camp of the Syrians: and when they were come to the uttermost part of the camp of Syria, behold, there was no man there.
2nd Kings 7:5

When you think about it, there is a risk attached to most things we do in life. If we sat down and thought about the risk of what could happen once we go out the door, we would never leave the house. We have seen how the lepers have carefully weighed things up and decided that going into the Syrian camp is worth the risk.

Just as you take a risk each time you leave the house, you also take risks when you step out in faith for God. The risk which Esther took was massive. Anyone who entered the king's presence without being invited risked being killed. While Esther took a life-threatening risk, she was not reckless and did what she could in preparation: she asked every Jew to fast for three days before seeing the king. People who take risks are not necessarily reckless. For example, those who climb Mount Everest take, at times, life-threatening risks, but they prepare meticulously for months. In the end, God's favour was upon Esther, and all was well.

As you *go through with God*, you will doubtlessly be brought into situations where you must take risks. That doesn't mean being reckless or taking those risks unprepared. It is so vital to bathe those potential risk situations in prayer and seek the Lord before you do anything. The most important thing is this: if you know God is calling you to take the risk, go.

You may be afraid in case you fail, but remember Peter, who took a tremendous risk by stepping out on the water. At least he took the step of faith. But when he took his eyes off Jesus and failed, the Saviour's strong hand picked him up. Trapeze artists in a circus take significant risks but have a safety net underneath. Jesus is your 'safety net.' 'Underneath are the everlasting arms' (Deuteronomy 33:27).

DAY 126

The Day That Pigs Fly?

For the LORD had made the host of the Syrians to hear a noise of chariots, and a noise of horses, even the noise of a great host: and they said one to another, Lo, the king of Israel has hired against us the kings of the Hittites, and the kings of the Egyptians, to come upon us.
2nd Kings 7:6

'I*'m away to play some golf.' 'What about that job in the house I've been asking you to do for the last two years?' 'I'll start it as soon as I get home from the golf.' 'The day you do that job for me is the day that pigs will fly!'*

We are returning to the king's right-hand man, who expressed unbelief that the next day (during a famine and siege of the city), food would be *dirt cheap*. His thinking was that the food couldn't come through the city due to the siege, so the only other way would be from above. He mockingly asked if the Lord was going to make windows in Heaven. In effect, he was saying the day that would happen would be the day that pigs fly.

This man was restricting God. He was *putting God in a box*. When we put God *in a box*, He has a habit of smashing out of that box and doing things in a way we never imagined. The thing about it was that God had already made *windows in Heaven* in the past. When God's people wandered in the wilderness, God provided bread from Heaven as manna, which rained down from the skies.

However, on this occasion, God didn't rain food from above. He did it a different way. He made the Syrian army hear the noise of a great multitude of troops and chariots, and they made a run for it, leaving all their food in the camp. Isaiah 40:13 brings us crashing down to reality by asking who will be an advisor to God? Who will instruct Him how to do things? When we pray (often without realising it), we sometimes tell the Lord how He should answer our prayer. Then we are disappointed when *our plan* doesn't seem to be working out! But it's not our plan; it's His plan. You will believe it *the day that pigs fly?* This is the God Who opens the Red Sea and makes the sun stand still. Don't doubt what God can do.

DAY 127

Telling Others

Then they said one to another, We do not well: this day is a day of good tidings, and we hold our peace: if we tarry till the morning light, some mischief will come upon us: now therefore come, that we may go and tell the king's household.
2nd Kings 7:9

When something amazing happens in our lives, our immediate instinct is to tell others. A heart bursting with joy wants other people to share in its gladness. In an earlier devotion, I mentioned how I proposed to Di. It was in a side room in Belfast Castle after a meal. There was an elevator in the room, and just as Di accepted my proposal, a group of people exited the lift. I hadn't a clue who they were, but I told them excitedly, *'We just got engaged! We just got engaged!'* They congratulated us and shared in our joy. Here's what I want you to think about. While that was an unforgettable moment, after sixteen years of marriage, I don't randomly stop people on the street and tell them that Di and I are married, expecting them to join in our joy! Maybe I should! As the Bride of Christ, however, we should be as passionate about telling others of Jesus as when we first got saved. Think back to the day you first trusted Jesus. You were so excited that you wanted others to know. But time passes, and we can lose that passion for telling others which we had at the start.

The four lepers are getting carried away with all the food they have been left with now that the Syrian army has fled the camp. Their people are starving in the city, and the lepers fear that something terrible may happen to them if they don't let the others know. Proverbs 11:26 tells us that if someone has enough corn but withholds it from his people, they will curse him. The lepers told the others out of duty and fear. We should want to tell others about Jesus out of love and compassion. How can we withhold the good news from others who desperately need it? Our fire will be ignited once again when we revisit Calvary and remember how Jesus first won our hearts through His amazing love for us when we did not even deserve it. Let that fire passionately burn as you tell others.

DAY 128

Don't Withold The Good News From Others

And he called the porters; and they told it to the king's house within.
2nd Kings 7:11

We will finish this section by examining yesterday's theme of telling others. First, we need to tie up a few loose ends. Elisha's incredible prophecy that prices would drastically drop the next day, came to pass. God is always faithful to His Word, no matter how impossible the thing may seem. Unfortunately, the chapter has a sad ending as the king's right-hand man (who mocked the Word of God) is trampled at the gate by the rush of people to get food. As prophesied by Elisha, he doesn't enter into the blessing. God's Words of blessing and judgment are fulfilled in equal measure. God means what He says. One day, the final judgment will fall on an unbelieving world, just as He said. But today, He promises salvation to those who will believe: 'Now is the day of salvation' (2nd Corinthians 6:2). Step out on that promise today if you have not done so already.

In today's verse, the lepers tell the porters about the food, the porters tell the king, and eventually, all enter into this wonderful blessing. The Christian life is a life of telling others. When we get saved, we tell others, and so it goes on. The Samaritan woman whom Jesus met at the well in John chapter 4 had been an adulterer. As Jesus dealt with her soul and told her of the unending supply of living water He could give, her heart was changed. And then it is as if fireworks go off in her soul. She immediately goes into her city, full of excitement. She has found their Messiah, but doesn't want to keep Him to herself, and brings the people of the city to hear Jesus. Later, we read that many Samaritans believed in Jesus due to the woman's testimony.

Due to the lepers' testimonies, the starving people come into the blessing which they have already personally received. You also have a story to tell. It is different from anyone else's and unique to yourself. Through your story, many can come into the blessing you have already so wonderfully received. Go and tell others.

SECTION 12

WAITING AND TRUSTING

2nd Kings 8:1-6

DAY 129

Disrupted Plans

Then spoke Elisha to the woman, whose son he had restored to life, saying, Arise, and go you and your household, and sojourn wheresoever you can sojourn: for the LORD has called for a famine; and it shall also come upon the land seven years.
2nd Kings 8:1

It was a Bank Holiday, and I took the afternoon off. We went to a park and had arranged to meet Di's Aunt Sheila for *fast food.* I had a strategic plan that would have us back in time to watch the climax of the *World Snooker Final*. However, it was suggested we should go to a Pizza restaurant instead. We arrived at 5.30 p.m., and the attendant said there would be *'a good forty-minute wait'* for a table. I joked: as long as it wasn't *a bad forty-minute wait*. I wasn't laughing for long. The pizzas were set down to us two hours later at 7.30 p.m. By the time we got home, it was 9 p.m., and the snooker was well underway (two hours). The whole point of the story is that we had plans made. A *curve ball* was thrown when someone changed our plans. This caused us to have to wait a long time until we could get back on track. It wasn't a big deal, but it is just a simple illustration to break you into this story.

Our passage returns to the Shunammite woman. Elisha's servant Gehazi (who was struck down with leprosy) appears also in this passage, which puts it chronologically before the story of Naaman. We will see a woman whose life is interrupted as Elisha speaks words that will throw a *curve ball* into proceedings. Her life is turned upside down, and her plans are wrecked. She would leave her country and wait seven years to return. I wonder, have words been spoken into your life which have disrupted everything? It could be your job, family, health or a host of other things that have been turned upside-down. Now, you find yourself in God's waiting room, waiting for things to change: waiting and hoping. Let me remind you that no one waits on God in vain. He hears your heart's cry. They that wait on the Lord shall renew their strength (Isaiah 40:31). *Remember, the waiting comes first, and then the mounting up with wings as eagles.* He can make you soar again.

DAY 130

Let God Direct Your Paths

Then spoke Elisha to the woman, whose son he had restored to life, saying, Arise, and go you and your household, and sojourn wheresoever you can sojourn: for the LORD has called for a famine; and it shall also come upon the land seven years.
2nd Kings 8:1

I'm sure you have seen on the news where there has been a hurricane warning somewhere across the world. Traders board up their windows, and families prepare to leave their homes until the storm passes. But you will usually find that there is someone who refuses to go. They say that they are prepared to ride out the storm. The emergency services pay a visit to inform the person that they are risking their life, but they refuse to leave.

Elisha has told the Shunammite woman there will be a seven-year famine. He instructs her to leave and go elsewhere. What would you have done? Would you have gone? Or would you have refused to go and try to ride out the storm? Back on *Day 47,* we saw that she could possibly have been a woman of great wealth. Could she not have weathered the storm if she was rich? Did she really have to do something as drastic as leaving the country? In the end, she obeys and goes to the land of the Philistines for seven years.

When important decisions come our way, we can be tempted to work things out ourselves. The Bible is very clear that the person who wants to *go through with God* will trust in the Lord with their heart and not lean towards their own understanding (Proverbs 3:5). This is the daily choice we must make. We cannot lean on our own understanding and lean on the Lord at the same time. One takes us down a separate path from the other. Proverbs 3:6 goes on to tell us that when we do acknowledge Him, He directs our paths. Sometimes, those paths may take us to places we don't particularly want to go. But our focus is not so much on the path itself but rather on the One Who leads us along the path. That's what trust is all about. Can you trust Him with your pathway?

DAY 131

An Early Warning

Then spoke Elisha to the woman, whose son he had restored to life, saying, Arise, and go you and your household, and sojourn wheresoever you can sojourn: for the LORD has called for a famine; and it shall also come upon the land seven years.
2nd Kings 8:1

Around the beginning of *'Covid-19,'* we had the strange phenomenon of people panic-buying toilet rolls because they thought there would be a shortage. When people hear that oil prices are rising, many will take the opportunity to fill their oil tanks before the price increases. If the weather forecast gives rain for the following week, some will cut the grass while the weather is still reasonable. When we receive an early warning of something which is forecast to happen, it gives us the chance to prepare and plan ahead.

The Shunammite woman is given an early warning by Elisha about a seven-year famine which is on the way, and she is able to make the necessary plans in good time to avoid it.

Thinking about this seven-year famine being foretold, I am reminded the Word of God warns of a seven-year tribulation coming upon the world. In Revelation chapter 6, Jesus opens the seals of the book, and the *four horsemen of the apocalypse* (as they are commonly known) are sent into the Earth. The third horse was black, representing famine. Jesus said that the tribulation which will come in those days will be so bad that there never has been anything like it in the past, nor will there be anything of its equal in the future (Matthew 24:21).

Jesus is coming again. He urges people to be ready (Matthew 24:44). The signs of the times worldwide surely scream out to us that we are getting closer to that day. Amos 4:12 instructs us to 'Prepare to meet your God.' Take advantage of the early warning Scripture has given us, and make your preparations to be ready for Jesus' return. If you are ready, then watch, work and pray, seeking to win others for Jesus. To be forewarned is to be forearmed.

DAY 132

Jesus Is The Prize

And the woman arose, and did after the saying of the man of God: and she went with her household, and sojourned in the land of the Philistines seven years.
2nd Kings 8:2

Di left Brazil's tropical climate in 2001 and arrived in Northern Ireland. On seeing our cold, wet climate, she definitely realised that *'We're not Brazil, We're Northern Ireland!'*[23] (That's a well-known football supporters' song title). Di also left behind family and friends. She seemed to lose out in many ways, but had the move confirmed by a Word from the Lord. She felt it was in God's plan. For the Shunammite woman, obedience to God meant she would lose out in many ways. We will see later that by moving away, she would lose her claim to her ancestral land and all the property she currently had. She will leave friends behind and move into a foreign country where she will be a complete stranger. Did she really have to go?

Often, obedience to God means we lose out in some way, although He often compensates us. Abraham seemed to lose out when he was told to leave Ur. He didn't even know his destination. But God gave him descendants more than the stars in the sky. It seemed the disciples had lost out when they left their fishing business and followed a penniless Rabbi named Jesus, but they ended up turning the world upside-down.

However, my mind has been directed to the often-forgotten heroes of Hebrews 11. At the end of that illustrious list, we read of those who were tortured, stoned, sawn in two, killed by the sword, persecuted and mistreated. They lost out and didn't seem to be compensated down here for their obedience. You see, obedience is a reward in itself. It's the joy of serving the One Who loved us so much. Jesus did His Father's Will, not for a reward, but because He loved to do so (John 14:31). Whether there is a reward or not down here, obey Jesus out of love. Our reward in Heaven will just be a bonus. Jesus is the prize.

DAY 133

Waiting Time Is Not Wasted Time

And the woman arose, and did after the saying of the man of God: and she went with her household, and sojourned in the land of the Philistines seven years.
2nd Kings 8:2

When I receive confirmation for something through Scripture, it often comes *not through one verse but three.* This has happened on at least three major occasions in my life. I joke that the Lord knows I need to be told three times for it to finally sink in! One of those occasions was when I was praying for God to lead me to the person He had for me to spend my life with. I received three verses of confirmation (in short succession) that God had someone for me. I didn't know I would have to wait twelve years for her to show up! Through the plan of God, He took someone from a country of over 200 million (Brazil), brought her over here, and the rest is history. Di and I recently celebrated our sixteenth anniversary. In those twelve intervening years, was I totally at rest that all would work out? Unfortunately not. There were times of doubt: was I sure I had heard from God? Why is it taking so long? In the end, Di was worth the wait! But waiting was the hard part.

If we had been in the position of the Shunammite woman, how would we have reacted to the waiting time of seven years? Would we have questioned if we had made the right decision? Would we have wondered should we go back home early, perhaps after three or four years? Waiting on God can be so difficult. We want Him to operate on our schedule, forgetting He has a much grander plan. Abraham had to wait twenty-five years for God's promise of a son in his old age to be fulfilled. There was no sign of a son in the intervening years, so he and Sarah tried to speed God's promise up, but that didn't work out too well. In His own time, God fulfilled His promise. Those who *go through with God* must learn to wait on God. *Waiting is not wasted time.* Tomorrow, we will see that waiting time is trusting time, drawing us closer to God.

DAY 134

Waiting Time Is Trusting Time

And the woman arose, and did after the saying of the man of God: and she went with her household, and sojourned in the land of the Philistines seven years.
2nd Kings 8:2

Being in a doctor's waiting room can be very frustrating. It seems that the names of everybody in the room are called to see the doctor, except your name. So, you start to tap your feet in impatience and pick up a magazine to try and focus. But your eyes just follow the words, and you are not taking anything in. You attempt to distract yourself by reviewing in your mind the various symptoms you have experienced (as you are going to be asked what they are), but the more you think about them, the more anxious you become. By now, you just want to get home. You get up to leave, and your name is called!

As we continue to think of this woman who waited for seven years, how does a person wait on God? Tapping our feet impatiently (as in the doctor's waiting room) is not waiting on God. In Psalm 40:1, David says he waited patiently for the Lord. *Waiting time is trusting time.* It's like that faithful dog who sits every evening at the front door at 6 p.m., wagging its tail, waiting patiently for its owner to come home. Sometimes, animals can be more patient and faithful than humans!

Waiting can make us anxious as we worry about how things will pan out. Paul reminds us not to be anxious but to make our requests known to God. When we tell the Lord how we are feeling and give our concerns to Him, we can be assured that His peace, which passes all understanding, shall keep our hearts and minds through Jesus (Philippians 4:6-7). From that, I would expect that when I commit something to God, I will have an extraordinary peace come upon me that I would not have if I hadn't looked to the Lord. In those moments of waiting, we cannot expect God's total peace unless we commit our moments to Him. Wait patiently for the Lord and experience His extraordinary peace as you trust Him.

DAY 135

God Is Working While You Are Waiting

And it came to pass at the seven years' end, that the woman returned out of the land of the Philistines: and she went forth to cry to the king for her house and for her land.
2nd Kings 8:3

As I look back over the approximately forty years of Dad's illness (from around 1971 until his Home call in 2011), there were many distressing moments. There were times when it seemed we, as a family, were constantly moving from one crisis to another. But we can truly testify that God was faithful through it all. Following Jesus doesn't mean life will be without its struggles, but it does mean you prove through those difficult times that you have One Who stands by your side: the true, faithful God.

It is interesting to compare this story in 2nd Kings 8 with that of Naomi (from the book of Ruth). Both women left their homeland due to famine and went to another country (Naomi to Moab, the Shunammite woman to the Philistines' land). Noami came home as a broken and bitter woman due to the death of her husband and two sons while in Moab. The Shunammite woman will return to her homeland with no house or land to call her own. She had lost them through being obedient to God. They both return empty, but God proves His faithfulness to both women. Their story is not over yet. Naomi will be blessed through Ruth's new husband, Boaz, and the Shunammite woman will have her land restored.

I don't know the details of your story, but if you are a believer in Jesus, He will take care of you. There will be storms in your life (they come to everyone), but God will remain faithful. While you are waiting, God is working in the background. As Naomi wearily made her way home from Moab, she did not realise that Boaz was waiting for Ruth and that God would look after them. As the Shunammite woman travelled home, not knowing where she could live, Gehazi was talking to the king about the miracle Elisha had done in her life. This led to the restoration of her property. God is working in the background of your life, too. He is faithful.

DAY 136

Coincidence?

And it came to pass, as he was telling the king how he had restored a dead body to life, that, behold, the woman, whose son he had restored to life, cried to the king for her house and for her land. And Gehazi said, My lord, O king, this is the woman, and this is her son, whom Elisha restored to life.
2nd Kings 8:5

Emma (I have changed names for sensitivity) was disturbed by a dream in which Ruby was crying and in great distress. Emma felt led by the Holy Spirit to pray for Ruby. The next day, Emma contacted Ruby to find out how she was keeping. She mentioned that she had dreamt about her. Ruby opened up. That previous night, when Emma had the dream, Ruby and her husband had decided to end their marriage and to divorce. This came as a complete shock to Emma as there was no indication the marriage was heading in that direction, but she was able to offer support and comfort at that time. There are no coincidences with God. He knew that Ruby needed someone to be there for her at that very moment.

The Shunammite woman had to leave Israel due to famine and went to the land of the Philistines for seven years. On leaving her homeland, she forfeited her house and land. As she returns home, Elisha's servant, Gehazi (this incident must have happened before he was struck down with leprosy), is speaking to the king. Now, isn't that a coincidence (or is it)? The king asks him to recount the miracles of Elisha. Gehazi tells how the Shunammite woman's son had died and of God's power, which restored him to life. At that point, the Shunammite woman walks in and pleads to the king for her land. This incident will lead to the restoration of her land.

Things happen in our lives that the world would usually label as coincidences, but we know beyond the shadow of a doubt to be the hand of God. This comes within the framework of Romans 8:28, where we read: 'And we know that all things work together for good to them that love God, to them who are the called according to his purpose.' Coincidence? No, it is God at work.

DAY 137

Worth Restoring

And when the king asked the woman, she told him. So the king appointed to her a certain officer, saying, Restore all that was hers, and all the fruits of the field since the day that she left the land, even until now.
2nd Kings 8:6

I reversed the car and hit the wall behind me. There wasn't a lot of damage, just a line that went across the bumper where it had been hit. The safety of the car was not affected in any way, and was still totally roadworthy. However, the car was now fifteen years old, and it wasn't worth fixing the bumper. You see, we usually judge whether or not to restore something, based on its worth.

The Shunammite woman discovers that God is interested in restoring to her what she had lost because of her obedience to Him. She had paid the price. She had *gone through with God* and seemingly lost everything. God now honours her obedience.

We also read in the Bible about Mephibosheth (Jonathan's son), to whom David restored the land he had lost. Mephibosheth didn't think he was worth restoring. He viewed himself as a 'dead dog' (2nd Samuel 9:8). However, Mephibosheth received restoration based on a covenant rather than his worth. Through this covenant, David had promised to look after Jonathan's family should anything happen to him. Covenants in those times were usually ratified by the shedding of blood.

As sinners, we are unworthy to stand before a Holy God, but He can restore what we lost through Adam because of a covenant made through Blood: the Blood of His Son, Jesus Christ. I felt that my car was not worth paying the price to restore the bumper, but God thought it worthwhile to send His Son Jesus to pay the price for your sins and mine. God is the great restorer. Psalm 23:3 says that He restores my soul. Joel 2:25 speaks of God restoring the years that have been wasted. There is no situation too hard for God. Place yourself in the Potter's hands and watch as He remoulds and restores you by His grace.

DAY 138

Restoration With Interest Added

And when the king asked the woman, she told him. So the king appointed to her a certain officer, saying, Restore all that was hers, and all the fruits of the field since the day that she left the land, even until now.
2nd Kings 8:6

We have journeyed with the Shunammite woman on two occasions. In chapter 4, through the power of God, Elisha restored her son to life. Now, in chapter 8, her land, which she lost when she obeyed God, has also been restored. There is no limit to God's grace. He loves to give and give and give. But God still hasn't finished. We read that not only was the land restored, but she was given interest on top of it. While she had been away for seven years, her land had reaped harvests. She was given what she was owed from the ground also. God is able to do more than we can ask or even think (see Ephesians 3:20).

As we saw yesterday, when God saves us, He restores all we had lost through Adam. But not only does the Lord do that, He has given us even more than what Adam had. God had communion in the Garden of Eden with Adam, but he could never speak of Christ living in Him (Colossians 1:27). Adam was master over all the animals of the Garden; we have been made joint heirs with Christ and will reign with Him forever. The untold blessings that we have come into through Jesus Christ are innumerable. One more thing: although Adam would never have known what suffering and sin were (before the fall), he also never knew what it was for God the Son to leave Heaven and die on a cross for him. We have experienced a Divine love Adam could never have experienced.

You will notice that the favour of God was on the Shunammite woman. She accessed the king's presence, where Gehazi was already speaking about her. Then, the king appointed a special officer to deal with her case. I want to remind you that as God's child, His favour is upon you. His grace and mercy flow like a river over you today. You are the apple of His eye (Psalm 17:8).

SECTION 13

THE SKY'S THE LIMIT

2nd Kings 13:14-21

DAY 139

Fill The Vacuum For Someone Else

Now Elisha was fallen sick of his sickness whereof he died. And Joash the king of Israel came down to him, and wept over his face, and said, O my father, my father, the chariot of Israel, and the horsemen thereof.
2nd Kings 13:14

I can see the picture so clearly in my mind. I would run in from school, go up the stairs and burst into Dad's bedroom to tell him something. He would be sitting in that big red hospital chair he had been given, and more often than not, his eyes were closed, and his lips were moving. He was praying: no doubt, praying for others, but more specifically, praying for Lynne's and my salvation. I am so thankful those prayers were answered. Lynne was actually saved two days after me, and that was a time of rejoicing.

Fast forward to 28th May 2011 and a hospital bed in Craigavon, and Dad's time has come. I leaned over him and whispered the words of the hymn, *'Face to face with Christ, my Saviour, face to face, what will it be? When with rapture I behold Him, Jesus Christ, Who died for me.'* [24] Not long after, Dad closed his eyes and opened them, face to face with the Saviour Whom he loved and served. Some days later, when everything was over, as I recollected that no one had ever prayed so intensely for me as Dad, I realised I would really miss those prayers so much.

King Joash is now the king of Israel, and on hearing that Elisha is dying, he comes to see him and weeps over his face. Generally speaking, Joash was not a good king (2nd Kings 13:11), and his weeping could have partly been because he needed the man of God to be alive, as he was worried about the Syrian army. He needed someone to call on God on behalf of Israel. Elisha's passing would leave a vacuum. I believe we all need someone whom we can depend upon to intercede with intensity on our behalf. Seek the Lord as to whom you can come alongside and be that godly influence in their life. Fill that vacuum for them. It could just make all the difference.

DAY 140

Genuine And Authentic

Now Elisha was fallen sick of his sickness whereof he died. And Joash the king of Israel came down to him, and wept over his face, and said, O my father, my father, the chariot of Israel, and the horsemen thereof.
2nd Kings 13:14

I heard a story about a preacher in Northern Ireland who was having gospel meetings in a local Town Hall. There were a few troublemakers lurking around, threatening to make mischief. An unsaved man, known locally as a *tough guy,* stood at the door. He said the first one to cause any trouble at the meetings would be flattened. No one dared. Although not saved at the time (he would get saved later), he knew the gospel was true and wouldn`t let anyone else say anything against it.

King Joash (as I pointed out yesterday) was generally not a good king. But he did have respect for the man of God, Elisha. You will remember that when Elijah was leaving this world, he told Elisha that if he saw him ascend to Heaven, then his request for a double portion of his spirit would be granted. As Elijah ascended, Elisha cried out, *'My father, my father, the chariot of Israel, and the horsemen thereof'* (2nd Kings 2:12). This indicated that he had seen Elijah go up to Heaven and was granted his request. Strangely enough, King Joash quotes those words as he weeps over Elisha. You see, despite the fact that King Joash is far from God, he recognises Elisha as a man of God. Even though Elisha speaks the Word of God without fear or favour, the king respects him. He knows he has that anointing of God upon him.

There are people in your life who may not be saved, but respect your testimony. They know you are genuine and can see that you have decided to *go through with God*. There is something different about you. They observe an anointing upon you. We normally think of the demonstration of the Spirit in terms of power, but there is also power in a smile, a kind word, godly advice, a listening ear, and so many other ways. The world desperately needs to experience genuine, authentic followers of Jesus.

DAY 141

Cancel Culture

And Elisha said to him, Take bow and arrows.
And he took to him bow and arrows.
2nd King 13:15

We live in a *cancel culture*. People are ostracised and ignored because they are deemed to have gone too far in what they have said or done. The 'standards' set by those doing the cancelling are based on *their definition* of 'standards.' The bar which they set may be low, high, or completely distorted. In the past, it was usually businesses which were boycotted, but now cancel culture takes in individuals also. There is the danger that this can happen in church circles, with a lack of grace shown towards others we don't see eye to eye with.

When this ungodly king comes to Elisha and weeps over him, he doesn't turn him away. Elisha doesn't *cancel him* based on what he knows about him. He shows grace. It is generally accepted that Elijah's life is a picture of *the law*, but Elisha's life is a picture of *grace*. Elisha doesn`t turn the king away but goes further, and is going to speak into his situation about his concerns over the Syrian army. Elisha is prepared to give the king a chance.

Jesus gave Judas chance after chance. He knew what was in Judas' heart, yet afforded him the same opportunities as the other disciples. He travelled with Jesus, saw His miracles, heard His teaching and was one of the most privileged men of his time. Even towards the end, as Jesus washed the disciples' feet, it seems Judas was still among their number (John 13:2-17).

We have all been in a position where someone has given us a second, third or even fourth chance. We have all been in a place where grace was shown to us when the opposite could have been the outcome (this, of course, is what God has done for us, but I speak specifically here of people). Those who *go through with God* will seek the heart of God. Today, you may encounter someone who needs to be shown grace instead of being *cancelled*. Be that grace-giver. *Compassion speaks louder than cancellation.*

DAY 142

Put Your Hand On Someone's Hand

And he said to the king of Israel, Put your hand upon the bow. And he put his hand upon it: and Elisha put his hands upon the king's hands.
2nd Kings 13:16

Granda Seifert would have preached with his father and my Dad (before Dad took ill), and the gospel was close to his heart. I will never forget the last time I saw Granda before he died. It was in the hospital along with my sister, Lynne. Granda wouldn't have overly shown public displays of affection (like many men), but I will never forget how he took my hand and Lynne's in his. Then he said, *'Isn't it time you and Lynne were thinking about getting saved?'* We did not see him again. That touch of his hand on mine, his words (which sought to guide me to salvation) and then his subsequent death hugely contributed to my journey in seeking the Lord for salvation. He started me on that path.

Here we have this lovely picture of Elisha, the prophet of grace, taking this opportunity to guide this king into the right paths. Elisha has had a long ministry and is now an old man. You can see those old, experienced hands resting on the king's hands. Elisha had seen a lot in his life. He had witnessed the power of God first-hand. In the last act of his life, he wanted to pass on something to this wayward king.

Have you ever thought of mentoring someone? Who can you take under your wing and give some guidance or encouragement? What have you learned that you can pass on to others? What have you seen of the power of God that others need to know about? How can you gently come alongside someone, put your hand on their hand (spiritually), and encourage them to *go through with God?* Or maybe you are a younger Christian. Have you ever thought about coming alongside a more mature Christian and seeking to learn from what they have experienced in their walk with God?

We all need each other. We all can learn from one another. We all need someone to reach out a hand and show we care.

DAY 143

God's Hand On Ours

And he said to the king of Israel, Put your hand upon the bow. And he put his hand upon it: and Elisha put his hands upon the king's hands.
2nd Kings 13:16

There's nothing like a helping hand, especially when you are tired and weak. It makes all the difference. As you see this old prophet and his battle-ready monarch, you would think that King Joash's hands on the bow are most important. But it is Elisha's hands because they symbolise the hand of God. It is a picture of how needy this king is. He needs the power of God to help him. By placing his hands on the king's, Elisha indicates that God's power will indeed be with him in the upcoming battles with Syria. It is also a lovely picture of the hand of God working along with the hand of man. God was going to win the battles for Israel, but He was going to use even this weak king for His glory.

The message is very clear. If we are going to fight the good fight of faith, we cannot do it alone and dare not try it alone. If we are going to *go through with God*, we need the Lord to put His hand upon ours. We depend so much upon the power of the Spirit of God in our lives. Ezra 7:28 says, 'And I was strengthened as the hand of the Lord my God was upon me.' Oh, to feel the hand of God upon us as we fight life's battles. That sling which David held when facing Goliath was only a sling. But with the hand of God upon his hand, it became a mighty force that would take down a giant. Without the hand of God upon David, that giant would still have stood tall, threatening Israel.

Then, we also have this lovely picture of God working hand in hand with humanity. He doesn't need us. He has ministering angels who serve before His throne. This God, Who spoke the universe into existence, can so easily speak the Word, and His will shall be done. But we are given the privilege to work alongside the Almighty One, Who lovingly and powerfully places His hand upon ours. As you *go through with God*, ask Him to show His power by placing His hand on yours in whatever you do today.

DAY 144

Fire That First Arrow

And he said, Open the window eastward. And he opened it. Then Elisha said, Shoot. And he shot. And he said, The arrow of the LORD's deliverance, and the arrow of deliverance from Syria: for you shall smite the Syrians in Aphek, till you have consumed them.
2nd Kings 13:17

The *Concord Hymn*, penned by Ralph Waldo Emerson,[25] commemorates the initial battle (in 1775) of the American Revolutionary War. The opening lines focus on the first shot fired to open hostilities. Emerson speaks of those who *'fired the shot heard around the world.'* That shot changed the course of history. Elisha tells the king to open the window eastward and shoot an arrow. In ancient times, it was a custom to shoot an arrow or spear into the country that was intended for invasion. It was a declaration that hostilities had begun.[26]

As we come towards the end of this devotional, just as King Joash was given a window of opportunity, I want to give you one also. Looking over your Christian life, perhaps you feel it has been generally lukewarm recently, and you haven't been putting God first. I want to give you the opportunity to shoot that initial arrow, to commence (as it were) hostilities and make a declaration that by the help of the Holy Spirit, you will *go through with God*, whatever the cost. Maybe you haven't been lukewarm as such, but you just want to go deeper with God. Or perhaps you are seeking more power and overflowing of the Spirit in your life. Maybe you feel you need more fire in your prayer life or a deeper hunger for God's Word. Whatever it is, shoot that initial arrow right now and determine to *go through with God.* Record the date somewhere as the beginning of hostilities in this spiritual battle to *go through with God.* Please remember in a battle, there are highs and lows. Don't be discouraged when the battle goes against you. Keep leaning into God and seek the power of the Spirit. Fight the good fight. If you have never taken that initial step of salvation, turn to Jesus today and call on Him with a repentant heart. He will save you, and you can take that first step to *go through with God.*

DAY 145

The Sky's The Limit

And he said, Take the arrows. And he took them. And he said to the king of Israel, Smite upon the ground. And he smote thrice, and stayed.
2nd Kings 13:18

We have some strange sayings in English. Think about this: If you are *'under the weather'* because you have been *'barking up the wrong tree,'* there is no point in *'crying over spilt milk,'* and you shouldn't *'walk around with a chip on your shoulder.'* So just be as *'happy as a pig in muck,'* and it will be *'a piece of cake.'* Phew. What has all *that 'got to do with the price of fish?'* Today, we will be using some similar sayings.

Elisha initially told King Joash to fire an arrow out the window eastward (towards Syria). Elisha called it the arrow of the Lord's deliverance from Syria. In reality, the king was being told to commence hostilities with Syria, and the Lord would deliver Israel. Elisha then takes things a step further. He is going to be told, in effect, to *'go and knock yourself out.'* (I've never really got that saying. Apparently, it means to *'go for it'* and give it *'your best shot'*). The king obviously has more arrows and is told to also fire them into the ground. The indication is that the more he fires, the greater will be the victory.

We will see the outcome tomorrow, but for today, I want to think about this blank canvas that the king has been given. He has been encouraged to *'go for it.'* Basically, for the king, as he fires these arrows, *'the sky's the limit.'* When we pray to God, we are basically given a blank canvas, and as we shoot our prayers upward, *'the sky's the limit.'* Of course, we aren't guaranteed to receive exactly what we ask for; it is all subject to God's Will. The best thing we can do in that regard is to remember that the Spirit helps us when we pray (Romans 8:26-27). We can ask Him to guide us in what we should pray for and how we should pray. When you feel you have that leading of the Spirit, give your prayer all you have got. Aim high. *'The sky's the limit.'* Nothing is impossible with God.

DAY 146

Aim High

And he smote thrice, and stayed. And the man of God was angry with him, and said, You should have smitten five or six times; then had you smitten Syria till you had consumed it: whereas now you shall smite Syria but thrice.
2nd Kings 13:18(b),19

Our church had been praying for some time for a drummer. Around a year ago, those prayers were answered when a lovely couple came along. We gained not only a drummer but a violinist and singer. We only prayed for one position to be filled, but God gave us more than we asked for. I wonder what would have happened had we prayed for a full orchestra! (A spiritual rap on the knuckles for me)!

We left yesterday's devotional with a sense of expectation. King Joash has been told to shoot his other arrows out the window. The indication is that according to the number he fires, that will be the extent of the victory God will give him. Things take a sad turn because we see in this verse that Elisha is angry. Before we go any further, I must clarify that the king must have understood Elisha's test. Elisha would not have been angry if he hadn't understood. What happened? We read in verse 18 that the king fired three arrows and stopped. The indication is that he had more arrows, which he could have fired. He had a blank canvas ahead of him. The sky was the limit. But he stopped at three.

Although God assured the king he would have victory over Syria, the extent of the victory would be minimised by a lack of vision and passion for victory. He was content with three arrows. What would the outcome have been had he fired them all? We had a ministry which visited us recently that prints tracts and booklets. They started small but now print millions of pounds worth of literature worldwide. The amazing thing is that the whole operation is run based on faith. They step out in faith, and God provides. They weren't content with two or three arrows but fired all in their quiver! *Go through with God* and aim high in faith.

DAY 147

Jealous For God's Glory

And he smote thrice, and stayed. And the man of God was angry with him, and said, You should have smitten five or six times; then had you smitten Syria till you had consumed it: whereas now you shall smite Syria but thrice.
2nd Kings 13:18(b), 19

If you are doing a job, much depends on your state of mind. If you are really focused on getting the job done (and done right), and refusing to let anything get in your way, it is highly likely the end result will be a good one. However, if your heart is not in it and rather than seeking to give your best, you take a *'that will do'* approach (your goal being to do the bare minimum), things may not turn out so well. It seems that King Joash took the second approach as he was put to the test by the dying prophet.

As we have seen, the extent of Israel's victory would depend on how many arrows the king would shoot into the ground. Why did he stop at three? Was he discouraged or tired? Did he not understand what Elisha was doing? We saw yesterday that, based on Elisha's reaction, *he did understand.* In the end, it seems he had a lack of zeal for the glory of God. Three victories would be good enough for him. His heart wasn't really in it. In contrast, Elisha was jealous for God's glory and wanted to maximise the extent of the victory so the Lord would be exalted above His enemies. It should also have been Joash's desire to wipe the enemy out completely rather than give them a chance to come back for more.

How can we counter a laid-back approach in our service to God? A good outlook to have is one that longs to see God glorified. Jesus prayed in John 12:28, 'Father, glorify Your Name.' That was Jesus' deep desire in all that He did. Jesus didn't take a *'that will do'* attitude. Jesus gave His all in everything He did, so that God would be glorified. I wonder if we do things for God and our heart isn't really in it. Maybe we are discouraged or tired. *'Lord, help us smash through the barrier of how we feel today, and give us the ability and the focus to glorify Your Name in all we do. Amen.'*

DAY 148

The Man Who Went Through With God

And Elisha died, and they buried him. And the bands of the Moabites invaded the land at the coming in of the year.
2nd Kings 13:20

Operation *London Bridge* was the codename for the very meticulous funeral plans originally made decades ago should the Queen ever die.[27] In 2019, a false alarm went viral on a *WhatsApp* text when someone confused a drill for the real thing. Tributes began to flood in, but soon it was realised that Her Majesty was very much alive.[28] As we know, the code eventually came through that *'London Bridge Has Fallen,'* and on 8th September, 2022, Queen Elizabeth II passed away at the age of 96. The media went into overdrive. *Breaking News* banners rolled across TV screens. Archive film was played on a loop. The pageantry of the state funeral was watched by millions worldwide. A nation mourned.

When it came to Elisha's death, we simply read that he died, and they buried him. No pomp; no mention of great mourning for this powerful man of God. Why does it all happen so simply? John the Baptist spoke about Jesus: *'He must increase, but I must decrease.'* At the end of the day, Elisha was merely a servant of God who was obedient. The miracles were not his. They showed God's glory, not Elisha's. Although Elisha lived a life that demonstrated God's power, it was still a simple life marked by a resolute faith in the Lord. The Christian life is a simple one of faith and faithfulness. We may be carriers of the power of God; that does not make us superstars, but servants. Elisha never got carried away with the power; he did get carried away with serving God. That was his life ever since he burned that plough on his farm.

Elisha died, and they buried him. I think he would have been satisfied with that obituary. He didn't want celebrity status. He didn't want the miracles to be attributed to him. Elisha had done his work; now it was over. However, I think a fitting epitaph on his tomb would have been: *'The man who went through with God.'*

DAY 149

He Being Dead Still Speaks

And it came to pass, as they were burying a man, that, behold, they spied a band of men; and they cast the man into the sepulchre of Elisha: and when the man was let down, and touched the bones of Elisha, he revived, and stood up on his feet.
2nd Kings 13:21

We were standing in the vestibule of a funeral parlour when someone came in from the viewing room and said that a mobile phone was ringing in the coffin. It had accidentally been left inside and certainly startled those who heard it. It seems that the last chapter of Elisha's life has been written, and he fades into the background. But there is one almost bizarre episode to come. It is far more startling than a mobile phone left in a coffin. A dead man was thrown into Elisha's tomb, and when the body touched Elisha's bones, the man received back his life. This has got to be one of the most extraordinary miracles recorded in the Bible.

This incident reminds us that the miracles which Elisha did were not for his glory but God's. The prophet is dead; he didn't raise a finger or speak a word to perform this miracle. God performed this miracle through a dead body, just as he did through Elisha when he was alive. It was all of God. Dead men (or women) don't perform miracles. Neither do living men or women; God performs miracles *through* them as instruments who are yielded to Him.

One last thing. Elisha had asked for a double portion of the spirit of Elijah, and God granted his request. Elisha walked in the power of God, and even in death, that power was still evident. Hebrews 11:4 says: 'By faith, Abel offered to God a more excellent sacrifice than Cain….and by it he being dead yet speaks.' Even though he is long dead, Abel's faith speaks down through the centuries. Elisha was dead, but he still spoke. We can live in such a way that even when we have passed on, our lives and faith speak to those left behind. *Go through with God* and leave behind a testimony that others will see Jesus as they remember your life.

DAY 150

A Greater Miracle

And it came to pass, as they were burying a man, that,
behold, they spied a band of men; and they cast the man
into the sepulchre of Elisha: and when the man was let down,
and touched the bones of Elisha, he revived, and stood up on his feet.
2nd Kings 13:21

As you read this account of the man who came to life once his body touched Elisha's bones, could you imagine being there when it happened? Can you see the faces of those who witnessed it? Maybe you are amazed as you even think about it. We have good reason to be astonished when we read accounts of Jesus raising the dead and Old Testament prophets doing the same. It is probably the most impossible thing that anyone can think of, yet it happened. However, every day around the world, greater miracles are happening. Men and women who were sinners (once headed to a lost eternity) are saved by Jesus Christ, their sins wiped away, and their lives transformed and changed forever. That is by far the greatest miracle anyone could ever witness.

Here, a dead man's body comes in contact with Elisha's bones and receives life. In the same way, spiritually, someone who is dead in sins, when they come into contact with the effects of Jesus' death for us, they receive brand new life. What a miracle. Ezekiel 47:9 speaks of a river, and everything it touches brings life and healing. It is the same with Jesus. Whoever reaches out to Him in repentance and faith can receive life and healing. The woman in Matthew chapter 9, who pushed through the crowd, desired to touch the hem of His garment. Once she touched it, she was completely healed. What lost and broken people need today is to reach out and touch (by faith) the life-giving Jesus.

If you aren't saved or are a backslider, reach out and touch Jesus. If you long for a closer walk with the Lord, reach out and touch Him. His power is real. Once you feel the power of His touch, it will be like a fire that will create in you a deep desire to *go through with God. 'Lord, please send each of us that fire today. Amen.'*

Postscript

Maybe you have been reading this book and you are not a Christian. Perhaps you have been wondering how you can come into a personal relationship with Jesus Christ. Here are some pointers that may lead you to that place of blessing.

Realise that you are a sinner before a Holy God (*Romans 3:23*).

Recognise that sin separates us from God forever (*Romans 6:23*).

Repent of your sin (*2nd Peter 3:9*).

Recall how Jesus loved you so much that He died on the cross for your sins (*John 3:16*).

Request for Jesus to save you. Call on His Name (*Romans 10:13*).

Receive His free gift of salvation through faith (*John 1:12*).

Assurance of salvation comes through believing what God has said. Simply take Him at His Word (*1st John 5:13*).

Read and pray regularly to learn more about Jesus and come closer to Him each day (*Psalm 119:105*, *Philippians 4:6*).

Find a church that preaches the good news of salvation and fellowship regularly with other believers (*Hebrews 10:25*).

Seek the Baptism of the Holy Spirit for power to serve God. Witness to others and tell them about Jesus (*Matthew 3:11, 28:19*).

Make a public declaration of your faith in Jesus by being baptized in water. This does not save you, but comes after salvation. It is an act of obedience and a declaration of faith (*Acts 2:41*).

Perhaps you have been saved for a number of years but are not in that place that you know you should be. I would ask you to take a look in your 'mind's eye' to Jesus on that cross and remember what He did for you there. Remember His love for you. Come back to Jesus today and don't put it off any longer (*Luke 15:20*).

Jesus is coming again. Watch and be ready.

End Notes

INTRODUCTION

[1] Buffum, Herbert. 'I'm Going Through.' (Public Domain)

DAY 5

[2] House, P. R. (1995). *The New American Commentary; 1,2 Kings* (Vol. 8). (E. R. Clendenen, Ed.) Nashville: B & H Publishing Group.

DAY 6

[3] Bodner, K. (2019). *Commentary On 1-2 Kings.* (E Book Short Edition ed.). (Grand Rapids: Baker Publishing Group), 109.

DAY 10

[4] MacIntyre, R. G., & Davidson, A. B. (2020). *Study The Prophets: Elijah & Elisha.* (Kansas City: HQM Publishing House), 74

DAY 22

[5] MacIntyre, R. G., & Davidson, A. B. (2020). *Study The Prophets: Elijah & Elisha.* (Kansas City: HQM Publishing House), 74

DAY 29

[6] Warner, Anna. "Jesus Loves Me, This I Know." (Public Domain).

DAY 35

[7] Gardner, D. E. (2003). *The Trumpet Sounds For Britain. (Three Volume Edition)* (Southend-On-Sea: Jesus Is Alive! Ministries), 48-53

DAY 47

[8] Nelson, R. (1987). *First And Second Kings.* (Louisville: Westminster John Knox Press), 262.

DAY 50

[9] I tried in every way possible to discover the name of the writer of this chorus, 'The Move Is On' but was unable to find any records. From what I am aware, it is not usually required to do this for titles of songs or choruses, but I have endeavoured to do so to keep things right. From what I also understand, this chorus may be in the public domain by now, as it is quite an old one. I apologise if there is a name that is accredited to this chorus and will seek to rectify in any further printings of this book.

DAY 51

[10] Spafford, Horatio. "It Is Well With My Soul." (Public Domain).

DAY 59

[11] Konkel, A. H. (2006). *1 & 2 Kings.* (Grand Rapids : Zondervan), 561.

DAY 62

[12] Hubbard, Jr, R. L. (1991). *First & Second Kings.* (Chicago: Moody Press), 208

[13] Jones, H. (2012). *Philippians: For The Sake Of The Gospel* (Kindle Edition ed., Vol. 50). (Darlington: EP Books), Location No 1524.

DAY 68

[14] Coke, S. (1628). *The Institutes Of The Laws Of England.*

DAY 74

[15] Lamb, R. (1995). *The MacMillan Years, 1957-1963: The Emerging Truth.* (London: John Murray Publishers Ltd), 92.

DAY 82

[16] Moore, Dr. Clement C. "Twas The Night Before Christmas." (Public Domain).

DAY 86

[17] Norman, P. (2022, June 26). *Bicycle chains explained: everything you need to know*. Retrieved October 17, 2023, from Bike Radar: https://www.bikeradar.com/advice/buyers-guides/bicycle-chains/

DAY 103

[18] Navigators, T. (2011). *1 & 2 Kings.* Colorado Springs: NavPress.

DAY 106

[19] Lee, Jr., J. T. (2014). A Commentary On The Book Of Ephesians, Chapter Five. (Imprint: Independently Published), 103

DAY 108

[20] Spurgeon, C. H. (1899). *The Autobiography Of Charles H. Spurgeon.* (London: Curts & Jennings), 2:226-227.

DAY 111

[21] Warner, Anna. "Jesus Loves Me, This I Know." (Public Domain).

DAY 120

[22] *Hansard 1803-2005*. (1996, December 11). Retrieved October 17, 2023, from UK Parliament: https://api.parliament.uk/historic-hansard/written-answers/1996/dec/11/fuel-prices

DAY 132

[23] McAfee, Stewart. "We're Not Brazil, We're Northern Ireland."

DAY 139

[24] Breck, Carrie Ellis. "Face To Face With Christ My Saviour." (Public Domain).

DAY 144

[25] Emerson, Ralph Waldo. "Concord Hymn." (Public Domain).

[26] *Bible Commentary*. (n.d.). Retrieved October 18, 2023, from Biblia.Work: https://www.biblia.work/bible-commentary/exegetical-and-hermeneutical-commentary-of-2-kings-1317/

[27] DAY 148

Bostock, B. (2019, December 6). *A viral WhatsApp message that claimed the Queen had died...* Retrieved October 17, 2023, from Business Insider: https://www.businessinsider.com/news-queen-dead-accidenta-caused-confused-sailor-drill-2019-12?r=US&IR=T

[28] DAY 148

Ibid.

Other Titles

The author's first devotional book, 'Just A Moment' can be ordered directly through the following website:

www.malkoshpress.co.uk

For further information or to contact the author:
info@malkoshpress.co.uk

BVRSH - #0001 - 271023 - C0 - 229/152/11 - PB - 9781739201814 - Gloss Lamination